SOLITUDE AND COMMUNION

Papers on the Hermit Life
given at St David's, Wales in the Autumn of 1975

Edited by

A. M. ALLCHIN

SLG PRESS
Convent of the Incarnation
Fairacres   Oxford
OX4 1TB

A

ISBN 0 7283 0072 9
ISSN 0307-1413

CONTENTS

FOREWORD

THE ESSAYS printed in this book represent the larger part of the material prepared for the meeting on the solitary life which took place at St David's, Wales, at the end of September and the beginning of October 1975. Most of the papers published here were not read in their entirety during the meeting itself; they formed the basis for discussion and reflection in a conference which was planned to allow the maximum possible time for personal contacts, informal conversations, and long periods of shared silence and prayer.

The meeting was felt by all who took part in it to have been a remarkable and unlooked-for gift. The richness of the considerations, theological, spiritual and historical, and the deep underlying unity of vision which emerges from the very varied treatments of the subject to be found in these pages, were matched by a sense of personal enrichment and understanding on the part of all who lived those days together. The conviction, which motivated the original planning of the meeting, that this was a subject of unexpected importance, intimately linked with the most urgent spiritual problems of our own day, was more than confirmed in the event. It was not resolved to hold other meetings of precisely the same sort, but it was recognised by all that things had been seen, issues had been raised which, in various ways, will need to be taken further. Certainly the work of the Conference has not been without effect. The brief statement of principles made at the conclusion of the meeting, and printed at the end of this book, has already been incorporated, as an Excursus, into the newly revised *Directory of Principles and Practice* issued in 1976 for the guidance of the Anglican Religious Communities* by the Advisory Council for the Religious Life.

The life of the Christian solitary is one given by God and directed towards God in silence and anonymity. The lived reality of that way always goes beyond the words used to describe or direct it. There is, as

---

*The title of this revised edition is: *ANGLICAN RELIGIOUS COMMUNITIES, A Directory of Principles and Practice.*

all who took part in this meeting were vividly aware, an almost comic incongruity in convening a meeting to speak about a life given to solitude and silence. Yet, as both tradition and experience show, solitude and communion, silence and speech, support and strengthen one another. May these pages bear their own small witness to a way of life which itself bears witness alike to the mystery of God and to the mystery of man's heart called to contain nothing less than the uncontainable glory of the Divine Kingdom.

A. M. ALLCHIN
Fairacres, Oxford
Feast of St Athanasius 1977

THE SOLITARY VOCATION

SOME THEOLOGICAL CONSIDERATIONS

A. M. ALLCHIN

I WANT to begin with a very simple affirmation. I believe that the question which we have come to study here together during these days is one of vital importance not only for the whole Church, but for all mankind. We have come purposely to a place which seems marginal, and we shall be talking about a way of life which, in our time at least, seems particularly marginal. Yet, as I shall hope to suggest, the place of the solitary is only in appearance at the edge; in reality he is the one who stands at the very heart of things.

The place where we are meeting, St David's, itself may help us to understand a little more of this paradox. Geographically today it is remote and inaccessible, an eminently marginal place. In another age when, however difficult and dangerous sea travel was, it was at least less perilous than travel by land, its position was altogether different. It was one of the focal places of Celtic Christendom, a centre both of cenobitic and eremitic monasticism. In his poem, *The Last Sermon of St David*, Saunders Lewis, the greatest of living Welsh writers, brings to life again the medieval accounts of the saint's death. He draws our attention to the central place of David within the orders of the saints of Ireland and Wales. There is a gathering of the saints at the moment of his departure. But at the same time he vividly underlines the extreme simplicity, the bareness of the saint's injunctions as reported in his last sermon. 'Be joyful, keep the faith, and do the little things you heard and saw in me.' Here is at once the simplicity of the monk, and his place at the heart of the realm of spiritual realities.

In our time together we shall be considering our subject under three main headings:

1

a) Theological: how do we understand the place of the solitary way within the whole divine economy of creation and salvation?
b) Historical: how in fact has this life been lived out and understood in the different ages of the Church's history?
c) Pastoral and practical: what are the particular ways of prayer and discipleship which it involves; what are the ways in which it can most simply and most truly be lived now?

In this paper I shall be concerned primarily with the first question, but perhaps at the outset I may make a few very tentative preliminary remarks in relation to the historical and practical aspects of the matter. Historically it seems to me that the solitary life has had an absolutely central place within the tradition of the Church, once we free ourselves from thinking that the last four centuries of Western Christian history (Protestant and Catholic) are normative for our view of the whole. We are meeting in a place full of the memories of the first age of the Celtic Church, a Church eminently monastic, which held the hermit calling in the highest esteem. If we look on into the Western Middle Ages, we find, in a great variety of forms, that the solitary calling was still honoured and flourishing. Mother Julian of Norwich was not the only anchoress in the city of Norwich: more than fifty places where solitaries are known to have lived exist within the walls of medieval Norwich. And that is only one example. If we look to Eastern Christendom we find that at no time since the fourth century has the witness of the hermit been absent from the Church's life and consciousness, no less in the separated Churches, Coptic and Ethiopian for instance, than in the main body of Byzantine Christendom. In our century, as we know, many men and women here in Western Christendom have been led again to follow in this way. As an Anglican I feel in duty bound to mention the fact that in the very first community of Sisters to be founded in our Church in the mid-nineteenth century under the direction of Dr. Pusey himself, the Society of the Holy and Undivided Trinity, there was a Sister who lived for many years a life of almost total silence and solitude within the common life of the convent. She has not been without successors. Looking at the historical dimension as a whole one is struck by two things:
a) the importance of the hermit call through the Christian centuries;
b) the immense variety of ways in which the life has been led, and in which the solitary has been related to the Church as a whole, and to

the monastic community in particular.

For if we may come to the more practical and pastoral approach to the question, there are, I think, three elementary points which I should like to make:

a) The life is one which demands considerable maturity, human and psychological, as well as ascetic and spiritual. It is not a way to be undertaken unadvisedly, lightly, or wantonly, and it will not ordinarily be undertaken without some considerable experience of a regular life of prayer and obedience lived in community.

b) Following closely on this is the recognition that the life is one which has particular dangers, and which demands considerable capacities of spiritual discernment both in those who follow this way and in those who seek to guide them. For instance, some are by natural temperament attracted by solitude, and for them this calling may be particularly perilous—but also particularly blessed. Others are by natural temperament more sociable, and yet the Lord may call them apart. For them the dangers and the stresses will be different; the question of discernment may be, in some measure, easier.

c) Again, related to this is the vital recognition that each solitary is different. By the very nature of the calling there is something unique about each one. There are an indefinitely large number of ways of living the solitary life. This does not mean that there are no general principles underlying the life, nor does it mean that it will not be possible to discern a number of basic patterns of solitary life, largely measured by the degree of solitude involved and the forms of continuing association with the common life. It does mean, however, that it will be very difficult, indeed impossible, ever to legislate for and codify this way of life in a complete and systematic manner. Canon Lawyers must always admit themselves to some degree baffled at this point. Their categories will not finally be sufficient. And this fact is not an accident. It comes from the very nature of the vocation itself. And this brings us naturally to the main section of this paper.

I

LET US begin with our view of the nature of man. The world in which we live brings great pressure upon us to think of human beings as units,

3

numbers, replaceable and quantifiable. The whole technological and bureaucratic development of our society works in this direction. As machines become more and more important in human life, so more and more men are tempted to think of themselves in terms of cogs in a machine. This way of thinking of men and women as disposable units is not particularly new. We may suppose it to be characteristic of most previous human societies which were founded on slavery. But in our own times, which are in some ways freer, and which pride themselves on recognizing true human dignity, it takes new, less obvious and even more oppressive forms. Faced with this situation men think of themselves as individuals, parts of the whole, who have to assert their individuality over against the whole.

Such a view of man makes any deep understanding of Christian faith and prayer and life impossible. For God's revelation of himself in Christ and in the Spirit reveals to us not only the true nature of God, but also the true nature of man, made in God's image and likeness, personal and not individual. This distinction between person and individual has acquired particular importance in Christian thinking during the last hundred years. By man conceived as an individual, we refer to man conceived of as a small part of the whole, man who lives and survives by asserting himself against others, a creature who must either devour or be devoured. He can only become himself by separating himself from others; he can only become himself at the cost of others. This view of man is already propounded by Hobbes with great force in the seventeenth century. As a description of many of the features of fallen humanity, it has an unpleasant accuracy. As a description of the nature of man as created by God it is utterly false. For man is not an individual but a person. Not a replaceable part of the whole, but a unique and unrepeatable being in whom the whole (all humanity and indeed all creation) is mysteriously present. Man lives and survives not by asserting his own self against others, but by finding himself in and through others ('your brother is your life'). In freely giving himself to others he is not lost but renewed. He can only become himself in relationship to others, and far from this process of 'becoming himself' being at the expense of others, it is most profoundly with and for all others. In so far as the true nature of man, the image and likeness of God is being restored in anyone, just so far it is potentially being restored in all.

This view of man derives, of course, from a reflection on the mystery of God's self-revelation in Christ, and on the co-inherence of the persons within the life of the Godhead, and it is a vital presupposition for any living the solitary life. A person is one who recognizes the unity of his nature with that of all men. We can only grow into the uniqueness of our personal being by recognizing this common nature which we share. 'When thou seest the naked cover him, and hide not thyself from thine own flesh', says the prophet Isaiah. 'Whoever debases another debases himself', says a contemporary writer, James Baldwin. And the second great commandment is, of course, 'Thou shalt love thy neighbour as thyself'. And to love in this context means not to desire to dominate and possess, but to be willing to give oneself to the uttermost. This understanding of nature and person therefore is not a mere abstraction but a necessary tool for Christian living and praying, and it comes to us from our reflection on the very life of God in Trinity. The idea of a union which does not destroy the unique qualities of the beings united but brings them to perfection in uniting them comes from a reflection on the union of human and divine in Christ. And these considerations are essential for our view of the relation of each member of the Church to the Church as a whole. We shall never begin to understand the Church if we are thinking in terms of individuals and corporations. The Church is not an agglomeration of individuals—'a sandheap of individual perfections', in Father Congreve's words—but a unity of persons, the fellowship of the Holy Spirit. In the Church, as in the divine nature itself, the opposition of the one and the many is overcome, for the Church is placed within the creation as the image of the Trinity, the place where man is restored in his true nature in God's image and likeness. There are many persons but one body, many gifts but one Spirit, and the gifts are not divided out separately to each, but what belongs to each is common to all, and what is common to all belongs to each.

Such a vision of the Church, I repeat, is vital for the living of the solitary life. Without it the life of solitude would be a madness, or a kind of ultimate solipsism. But at the same time, without the life of solitude lived, and indeed understood within the Body of the Church, it will become increasingly difficult for the Church to retain this sense of her own nature. I do not know whether the comparative eclipse of the solitary life in Western Christendom was due to a comparable atrophying of this vision, or whether it was the decay of vision which followed on the obscuring of the way of life. I suspect that a study of history might show that it was the first and not the second. But what is clear already is that the two things go together. In our own century the recovery of the solitary life is profoundly linked with a number of other and at first sight apparently unrelated movements: liturgical, ecclesiological, and ecumenical.

Let us now illustrate the points which have been made from the work of a Western writer whose thought reflects faithfully the tradition of the Church in the centuries before the schism of East and West. St Peter Damian's 'Book on the Lord be With You' was written in answer to certain hermits who had enquired whether one might use the salutation, 'The Lord be with you', when saying the Office alone. Damian replies that they may:

> Indeed, the Church of Christ is united in all her parts by such a bond of love that her several members form a single body and in each one the whole Church is mystically present, so that the whole Church Universal may rightly be called the one Bride of Christ, and on the other hand every single soul can, because of the mystical effect of the Sacrament, be regarded as the whole Church.[1]

In his reading of the Bible, Peter Damian had noticed something which has attracted the attention of many modern biblical exegetes: the identification of the whole people with one man is so strong that the one may stand for the whole people.

> If we look carefully through the fields of Holy Scripture we will find that one man or one woman often represents the whole Church, for though because of the multitude of her peoples the Church seems to be of many parts [note the recognition of a plurality of peoples within the Church's unity], yet she is nevertheless one and simple in the mystical unity of one faith and one divine baptism. For indeed, although holy Church is divided in the multiplicity of her members, yet she is fused into unity by the fire of the Holy Spirit, and so even if she seems, as far as her situation in the world is concerned, to be scattered, yet the mystery of her inward unity can never be marred in its integrity. 'The love of God is shed abroad in our hearts by the Holy Ghost which is given unto us.' This Spirit is without doubt both one and manifold, one in the essence of his greatness and manifold in the diverse gifts of his grace, and he gives to holy Church which he fills, this power that all her parts shall form a single whole, and that each part shall contain the whole. This mystery of undivided unity was asked for by Truth himself when he said to his Father concerning his disciples, 'I do not pray for them alone but for them also who shall believe in me through their word, that they all may be one as thou Father art in me and I in thee,

6

that they also may be one in us that the world may believe that thou hast sent me.'[2]

Here is a vision of the Church, personal, sacramental and Trinitarian; a viewpoint full of consequence for our understanding of the element of multiplicity as well as the element of unity within the *Catholica*. We can see a close resemblance with that kind of eucharistic ecclesiology, developed in our own time by a number of Orthodox theologians, which insists on the fulness of each local church, united around its bishop, each one having in itself the wholeness of the Church's life, not being merely a part of the whole. But it is not only in each local church that the whole Church may be said to be present: it is in each member of the Church.

By the mystery of her inward unity the whole Church is spiritually present in the person of each human being who has a share in her faith and her brotherly love . . . Indeed, if we who are many are one in Christ, each of us possesses in him the whole, and though in our bodily solitude we seem to be far from the Church, yet we are most immediately present in her through the invisible mystery of her unity. And so it is that that which belongs to all belongs to each, and conversely that which is particular to some is common to all in the unity of faith and love . . . Now just as the Greeks call man a microcosm, that is to say, a little world, because his body is composed of the same four elements as the universe itself, so each of the faithful is a little Church since without violation of the mystery of her inward unity, each man receives all the sacraments of human redemption which are divinely given within the Church.[3]

If in Protestant theology (I do not say Protestant practice, for certainly in practice the solitary life has been and is lived within Protestantism) the hermit life has scarcely been envisaged, it is because this vision of the Church's nature has been generally absent. And if in Roman Catholicism since the sixteenth century, the hermit way has been less in evidence than hitherto, and hardly recognized in canon law, may it not be in part because such a vision of the Church, in which each member shares in all the sacraments of human redemption (Baptism, Confirmation, and Eucharist), has been overshadowed by other more juridical, clerical, and organizational views of the Church, forged in the heat of sixteenth and seventeenth century controversy? As long as the Church is conceived primarily in legal or institutional terms the solitary life will always appear as a threat to its unity and cohesion. The one will be thought of in contrast to the many, the solitary in contrast to the group. Only on the sacramental and personal view of things outlined here is it possible to see the coinherence of the two contrasting realities, to see the solitary as expressing the inward unity of the community.

We see here one of the many ecumenical significances of the solitary way; not only because it unites us all in a common adherence to a vision of God, man and the Church which was the shared heritage of the first thousand years of Church history, but still more because the hermit by his very life and call, lives the unity of the Church in a strikingly vivid and genuine way. 'A Christian hermit can, by being alone, paradoxically live even closer to the heart of the Church than one who is in the midst of her apostolic activities', writes one of the prophets of the eremitic renewal of our own day, Thomas Merton. 'Perhaps none have realised as intensely the saving mystery of fellowship, the love of brethren, as those whom God has called to live by prayer in the greatest solitude, even in the continual contemplation of the hermit', wrote one who was amongst the first theologians of the Anglican revival of the Religious Life in the nineteenth century, George Congreve. Those who appear marginal are in reality central. They live a form of life whose very meaning is an affirmation of unity. They live it in Churches which for many centuries have not been in canonical communion with one another. The particular poignancy of this situation is heightened when we remember the great role that the Churches which did not accept the decisions of Chalcedon had in the foundations of Christian monasticism, and when we recall that to this day, at least in Egypt and Ethiopia, this tradition of solitary life is still flourishing amongst them.

When we reflect how deep the influence of St Isaac of Syria on the spiritual tradition of Greece, Romania and Russia has been, we see something of the strangeness of this story. For the writer in question, one of the great exponents of the meaning of the solitary way was a bishop in the Nestorian Church, a Church for many centuries considered schismatic and heretical by the greater part of the Christian world. The divisions within Christendom are not of the last five or ten centuries alone. They go back into the first ages of the Church's life, and their meaning is perhaps different from what we usually take it to be.

8

II

SO FAR we have spoken of the solitary life in terms of man's creation by God in his image and likeness. And though we have not developed the line of thought at length, underlying our whole discussion has been the faith that it is not only mankind which is involved in this creative work, but the whole universe. The cosmic dimension of prayer and life is very strongly developed in the solitary tradition, expressing itself in many ways, not least in a particular closeness to the animal creation.

But the meaning of this way of life is to be apprehended not only in terms of God's purpose in creation. Its full significance begins to become apparent when we see it in relation to the work of redemption, when we begin to understand it in terms of the cross and the empty tomb. The solitary life is not only characterised by the quiet of the sabbath. It involves the single-handed conflict with the powers of evil, the way of the cross, which necessarily precedes entry into the peace of God.

I should like to quote from one of the last utterances of Derwas Chitty, a talk he gave at the Conference of the Fellowship of St Alban and St Sergius in August 1970, a few months before his death. The general theme of the Conference was 'Christian Responsibility in the World' and, very characteristically, Fr. Derwas chose to speak on the 'Calling to the Solitary Way' precisely in relation to this subject, for he saw the hermit as in some sense representative of us all. As he often did, he spoke in images rather than concepts. He evoked the two places which meant most to him on this earth, Bardsey Island off the tip of Lleyn Peninsula, and the Church of the Holy Sepulchre in Jerusalem, both of them places of meeting between man and God, both of them places of death and resurrection, both of them places where we find ourselves alone yet not alone.

First, the island of the saints: 'the island of hermits. The island of the solitude where one is least alone.' 'Each one who comes there seems immediately to make it his or her own. You don't need anyone else with you; you each do it in your own way. Everyone in a different way. But there you are.' And this which is perhaps true of every island was, we were reminded, specially true of this island where through the centuries men longed to be buried to await there the day of judgement. This understanding of the meaning of Bardsey, which Fr Derwas felt so deeply, was not a private fancy of his own. It is something which finds expression more than

once in medieval poetry, and most significantly in the last section of a poem
of Meilyr Brydydd.

> May I, the poet Meilyr, pilgrim to Peter,
> Gatekeeper who judges the sum of virtue,
> When the time comes for us to arise
> Who are in the grave, make me ready.
> May I be at home awaiting the summons
> In a fold with the moving sea near it,
> A desert it is of unfading honour
> With a bosom of brine about its graves
> Fair Mary's isle, pure island of the pure,
> The heir of resurrection, it is good to be in it.
> Christ of the foretold cross knows me, will keep me
> From the pains of hell, that place of exile.
> The Creator who created me will meet me
> In the fair parish of Enlli's faithful.[4]

These lines, which were very familiar to Fr. Derwas, come from a deathbed
poem of repentance and supplication written in the first half of the twelfth
century. There are many things in them which demand our attention. First,
how 'the fair parish of Enlli', namely, Bardsey Island, like St David's now
geographically remote, was then near the centre of things. Meilyr was
court poet to Gruffud ap Cynan, a prince of Gwynedd who after many
years of exile in Ireland managed to re-establish himself in North Wales.
It has traditionally been thought that he brought back with him from
Ireland strong influences in the realm of literature. Certainly his reign
coincides with the beginning of the second major period of Welsh poetry.
In such an Irish-Welsh perspective Bardsey, though always difficult of
access, lies close to the principle routes between the two islands.

Then we must notice that these lines, so full of insight into the meaning
of a holy place, are the work of one who was primarily a poet of war and
love, one who praised the prowess of the prince's warriors, and the beauties
of the ladies of the court. He was a man at the centre of his own small
world. His son Gwalchmai ap Meilyr, and his grandson Einion ap Gwalchmai,
succeeded him as court poets, and in the last named we find another poem
containing a prayer to be buried on Bardsey. We have here a reflection of
the attitudes of a whole society.

What is it that Meilyr sees about the meaning of the island? First it is
a place of seclusion. The word translated 'desert', in the original *ditrif*, is

one of the regular terms used in medieval Welsh for the dwelling of a hermit. And yet at the same time, the island is a place of assembly, of coming together, a place where one who is facing the solitude of death is supported by the communion of Mary and the saints. 'The island of solitude where one is least alone.' It is 'in the fair parish of Enlli's faithful', that he is to meet God. The use of the word parish (*plwyf*) is striking for the assembly of a monastic island, so closely are monk and layman associated in this vision of things, in this *solitudo pluralis*. Then, secondly, the island which is a place of death and burial, is at the same time the place of resurrection. Here we have one of the most remarkable and daring images in the poem. Having spoken of the island as Mary's isle, 'the pure island of the pure' (the word for 'pure' could equally well be translated 'holy'), he goes on to speak of it as 'the heir of resurrection' (*gwrthrych dadwyrein*). The word *gwrthrych*, which ordinarily means 'object' in Welsh, is used here in a technical sense to be found in old Welsh law to describe the heir to a king designated during his predecessor's lifetime. It may mean either 'the one who is in expectation' or 'the one who is expected'. In this case it would seem to be the former meaning which is the more appropriate. The island itself is in eager expectation of the resurrection of those who sleep within it.[5] All this, consciously or perhaps unconsciously, lay behind Fr. Derwas' feeling for Bardsey.

And then the Church of the Holy Sepulchre in Jerusalem. Fr. Derwas spoke of his many, almost daily, visits there when as a young man he was living in the holy city, unconsciously revealing something of the intense concentration of his own life on the person of the crucified and risen Lord.

Very early I tried to make a practice of going for a short time to the holy places each day. I did not manage it. . . . But, thank God, at least I tried to. Up on to that dark little Chapel which is Calvary. I would be there for quite a long time, going up and under the altar of Calvary and placing my arm through the hole in the plate underneath it to touch the bare rock on which the Cross had been set . . . A longer time generally on Calvary, and then a shorter moment going into the Sepulchre, the place of Resurrection, which is the central point, the key point of that church, where it comes as such a shock in a way for a westerner to find that Calvary is on one side, and the centre is the tomb. And we go and call it the Church of the Holy Sepulchre. But in the Greek it is the Church of the Resurrection, the reason why, indeed, the Sepulchre is at the centre, the place of Easter.

I have quoted at some length because the specific quality of the original needs to be savoured. It is all so factual, yet so universal. Bardsey, an actual place; Calvary, an actual place. 'Placing my arm through the hole'—both places of death and resurrection, both places of solitude and communion.

And to speak of the Cross. The Lord has moved among men. He has suffered, he has done his works of mercy. But where do you and I meet him? There, in those first words upon the Cross when he is looking out on those around him, 'Father, forgive them, for they know not what they do.' 'Today shalt thou be with me in Paradise.' 'Woman, behold thy son.' 'Behold thy mother.' It is after these that the darkness over all the land speaks of the soul of Christ going down into the depths of darkness and loneliness, utterly alone: 'My God, my God, why hast thou forsaken me?' In that word we find him closest to us, and know him to be God.

Here we find the paradox of *solitudo pluralis* at its starkest. In the hour of desolation, the Lord is nearest to us and to all men. Then, having evoked the experience of the risen Christ as he has made himself known through the centuries of the Church's history from the apostles until today, Fr. Derwas went on to make the link between the Cross, the tomb, and each Christian—indeed each man—in his solitude before God, explicit by a reference to the pillar saints of Syria, men who adopted one of the most scandalous and public forms of solitary life ever to be known in this world. 'The pillar of one who is as fixed to his place of prayer as the Lord is fixed to the Cross, and there is no going back.' And that mounting of the pillar was itself understood as a mounting of the Cross, 'after all the training . . . of the life in common, the entry into the quiet of that solitude.' So, through the conflict, we pass in the power of the Cross into the quiet of the tomb, the place of new life. And out of this identification with 'the Christ upon the Cross, the Christ in the darkness, the Christ in the loneliness', there comes paradoxically but at once a new discovery of our fellow men.

What is the nearest way from me to my brother? The closest of human attachments must always recognise, if it is honest, the clear line of separation which sets the boundary between two souls . . . But there is a shorter way from my soul to my brother's. The Christ by his Holy Spirit is in the innermost shrine of your heart and mine. There, where I do not penetrate, in that Holy of Holies, where the Holy Spirit is enthroned in our baptism, there he is. And when we reach him there, we are closer to every soul of our brothers than we can be in any other way... And when we are serving our brothers and sisters in everyday life, there is something missing in our way of doing it unless somewhere at the roots of our being there is that prayer which turns inward to the Christ and finds him there, and by doing so, we are enabled to look out and see them and see the Christ in them, and see the Christ looking in upon us through the eyes of those around us. Not only those who are outwardly and consciously Christian, but everyone whom he loves ...

So it is that in our own time the life of the hermit in some way makes present to us the supreme paradox that it is in the moment of utmost isolation and complete apparent uselessness, in the desolation of the Cross, that the Lord is able to bring about the atonement and reconciliation of man with God. That it is when he is lying dead in the tomb that 'all creation is moving in him'. We are reminded of the word of the Lord to Staretz Silouan, 'Keep your mind in hell and despair not.' We are reminded of the apparent utter failure of Charles de Foucauld dying in his desert hermitage, and of the way in which life has come forth from that tomb. We are reminded in our own Anglican tradition of the strange parallel in the life of Fr. William of Glasshampton. All that St Paul says about our dying and rising with Christ, our union with him in his death no less than in his resurrection, which is true for every Christian—in some sense, indeed, for every human being—is true in their specific measure for those who are called into the particular confinement of this narrow way. The Cross is outside the city, the tomb is in a hidden garden; but indeed they are at the true centre of the world.

III

WE HAVE considered the solitary life in relation to man's creation in the image and likeness of God, and his redemption through the death and resurrection of Christ. We must now come to consider our subject in relation to the work of the Holy Spirit, in his coming into the world at Pentecost. We have already had a clue as to this action of the Holy Spirit in the passage which was quoted from Peter Damian:

For indeed, although holy Church is divided in the multiplicity of her members, yet she is fused into unity by the fire of the Holy Spirit . . . This Spirit is without doubt both one and manifold, one in the essence of his greatness and manifold in the diverse gifts of his grace, and he gives to holy Church which he fills, this power that all her parts shall form a single whole, and that each part shall contain the whole.

There is within the Church a principle of unity and a principle of diversity or, we may say, a unity of nature expressed in a diversity of persons. The unity which the Spirit brings is not one which suppresses the true diversity of gifts, abolishing the uniqueness of each human person. Precisely the reverse is true: it is in the gift of the Spirit freely imparted and received that each one is established in the uniqueness of his own particular way. Amongst contemporary theologians few have written more illuminatingly on this subject than Vladimir Lossky, and though we need not commit ourselves to every detail of how he works out the relationship between the economy of the Son and the economy of the Spirit in the Church, we can certainly learn from the balance and insight with which he treats the matter.

Lossky presupposes the kind of distinction between personal and individual which we have already made:

> In the measure in which he is a person in the true theological sense of the word, a human being is not limited by his individual nature. He is not only a part of the whole, but potentially includes the whole, having in himself the whole earthly cosmos, of which he is the hypostasis. Thus each person is an absolutely original and unique aspect of the nature common to all.[6]

And it is precisely in relation to man's personal response to the word of God which calls him into being from nothing that this uniqueness needs to be stressed. We become the true and unique persons we are created to be, not in any attempt to assert ourselves or maintain ourselves by ourselves, but by going out of ourselves in love to God. For, says Lossky, 'it would appear that there are as many unions with God as there are human persons, each person having an absolutely unique relation with the Divinity . . .'[7] And it is the work of the Holy Spirit, who gives different gifts to each, to realise in each this unique calling.

If our individual natures are incorporated into the glorious humanity of Christ and enter into the unity of his Body by baptism, conforming themselves to the death and resurrection of Christ, our persons need to be confirmed in their personal dignity by the Holy Spirit so that each may freely realise his own union with the Divinity. Baptism—the sacrament of unity in Christ—needs to be completed by chrismation— the sacrament of diversity in the Holy Spirit.[8]

The relevance of this to the life of solitude is not far to seek. The one who is called to such a life needs to be one, above all, who is realising this personal vocation, realising, that is, both the profound unity and solidarity of all those who share in the body of Christ, and at the same time the extreme diversity of response called for by the grace of the Spirit which works in many ways and at many different levels. Speaking of the Church's awareness of the truth which it confesses, Lossky insists that this is not 'a "supra-consciousness" belonging to a collective person'. Rather, he maintains, 'there will necessarily be a multiplicity of consciousnesses, with different degrees of actualisation in different persons, more intensive in some, practically absent in others. Persons who are more deeply rooted in the Church, conscious of the unity of all in the Body of Christ, thus are more free of their own individual limitations, and their personal conscious- ness is more open to the Truth.'[9] Hence it may be in a moment of crisis for the Church, that the faith of the whole, the Catholic faith, will be realised in the *one*, an Athanasius or a Maximus, who has to stand against the overwhelming majority who have become blind to the truth.

To say that the call to the solitary life is a gift of the Holy Spirit in the Church is to say very little and yet to say everything. For in the coming of the Spirit, each one of us is established in his own, unique personal way towards God, through this most intimate, interior and self-effacing presence of the Lord the Comforter, at the very heart of our being. And this most mysterious and inward aspect of the Church's faith is signified and made plain in a special way by those who are called to live their solidarity with their fellow-men in silence and solitude. There is need here for a very deliberate reciprocity between those who follow this way and those who are called to the sacramental hierarchy of the Church, itself also a gift of the Holy Spirit. The life of one who lives in great isolation, cut off for long periods from any outward participation in the sacramental life of the Church, is likely to appear a scandal to those who have failed to measure the true nature of the diversity of callings within the Body. But at the same time, and more profoundly, it may be seen as a witness to the constant presence and power of the Holy Spirit, who is 'everywhere present and filling all things'; and as a rebuke to the Church's temptation to submit the freedom of her members 'to a kind of sacramental determinism', while itself constituting a kind of sacramental representation of the freedom which the Spirit gives to each one of us to grow up into our adoption in Christ, sons in the Son, children of the one Father.

CONCLUSION

I have spoken about the solitary life in relation to the life of the Church and of all mankind, and I hope to have suggested reasons why the vocation of the one who is summoned to live in physical solitude is of the utmost importance to all his fellow-men in helping them to understand and discover that dimension of solitude which lies at the heart of every life. About the solitary life in itself I have not ventured to speak, being in no way qualified to do so. I should prefer to conclude with the words of a true hermit—Thomas Merton—which may act as a corrective to any tendency to put too much trust in formulations.

> The solitary life is an arid, rugged purification of the heart. St Jerome and St Eucherius have written rhapsodies about the flowering desert, but Jerome was the busiest hermit that ever lived and Eucherius was a bishop who admired the hermit brethren of Lérins only from afar . . . The true solitary is not called to an illusion, to the contemplation of himself as a solitary. He is called to the nakedness and hunger of a more primitive and honest condition. The condition of a stranger and a wanderer on the face of the earth, who has been called out of what was familiar to him in order to seek strangely and painfully after he knows not what.[10]

NOTES

1. St Peter Damian, *Selected Writings on the Spiritual Life*, trans. Patricia McNulty, Faber, 1959, p.57.   2. Ibid pp.58-9   3. Ibid pp.63-4.

4. An English translation of the whole poem may be found in Joseph P. Clancy, *The Earliest Welsh Poetry*, 1970, pp.117-8. See also Gwyn Williams, *An Introduction to Welsh Poetry*, Faber 1953, p.73. The translation given here is adapted from Gwyn Williams'. (Enlli is the Welsh name for Bardsey.)

5. I am deeply indebted to Professor Idris Foster for help in the exegesis of this poem. On the meaning of *gwrthrych* see D.A.Binchy, *Celtic and Anglo-Saxon Kingship*, Oxford 1970, pp.27-28.

6. Vladimir Lossky, *In the Image and Likeness of God*, Mowbrays 1975, p.107.

7. Ibid p.105   8. Ibid p.108.   9. Ibid p.192

10.Chapter 'The Philosophy of Solitude' in *Disputed Questions*, Hollis & Carter 1961, p.198.

16

SOLITUDO PLURALIS

DOM ANDRÉ LOUF O.C.S.O.

THE TITLE of this article is borrowed from a famous little work by St Peter Damian entitled *Dominus Vobiscum* in which the author makes a detail of liturgical observance the excuse for developing a remarkable doctrine on the place of the eremitical life in the Church.[1] The expression *solitudo pluralis*—corporate solitude—will suggest to us a few thoughts on the community implications of a Christian vocation to solitude.

The problem troubling the hermit to whom Peter Damian was replying is not a disturbing one: has one who celebrates the Office in solitude the right to pronounce *Dominus Vobiscum*, 'The Lord be with you', or not? If he has, why? And how is it to be understood? Is he not bound in that way to 'wish the Lord's presence upon the stones or the furniture in his cell?' It is therefore a question of what today we should call a problem of the truth of the celebration of the liturgy. We have become particularly sensitive to it.

Peter Damian's answer is simple and clear. The hermit not only has the right to use the customary words of the liturgy, but it is absolutely necessary that he should do so, and without fail. Firstly, because these words are obligatory; secondly, and above all, because they express a deep reality of his life: even when alone the solitary is never isolated, he is always with others, his solitude is in some way necessarily corporate. By the adhesive of love, *caritatis glutinum*, the solitary is united with all his brothers and that in an almost sacramental way by the mystery of the sacrament, by inviolable sacramental unity—*per mysterium sacramenti, per unitatis inviolabile sacramentum*. In him are thus realized two basic qualities which the Church receives from the Holy Spirit: that which unites and that which diversifies. The Church is at the same time one and universal. She always comprises a complete multitude of persons, and reduces these to the unity of the Body of Christ. At the same time, at the point where

17

she lays hold of the individual, she brings him within the universality of the whole. She is at once solitary—for she is the sole bride of Christ—and multiple, for she must shine on all men. Her solitude must therefore be understood in the plural, just as her diversity must be understood in the singular.

The conclusion of such a doctrine, with regard to the eremitical liturgy, is immediately obvious. What the hermit celebrates alone has repercussions on the whole Church: whatever is done during the holy Offices by any of the faithful *in particular* should be regarded as done by the Church, *joined together* in the unity of faith and the love of charity—*quidquid in sacris officiis a quibuscumque fidelibus* particulariter *agitur, hoc ipsa Ecclesia per unitatem fidei et caritatis amorem* unanimiter *agere videatur.*

In prayer, a strictly solitary action is no longer possible. Thanks to the sacrament of the Church, a kind of permanent proxy exists on behalf of every solitary. His commission is directed towards the Church as a whole. He is invested with an *officium universitatis.* The hermits, even when they are bodily far away, are very much present—*presentissimi*—to the Church. Inventing an expression which he is not ashamed of borrowing from what knowledge he may have had of Greek philosophy, Peter Damian goes so far as to say that the hermit may be called a *minor ecclesia* or micro-Church, a Church in miniature which, in communion with all the other members, already possesses within itself all the essential elements of its mystery.

It was, therefore, easy to resolve, without too many obstacles, the small problem of ritual which was submitted to him. At the same time, Peter Damian has just touched on one of the major problems of all eremitical experience, a problem on which he throws the light of his powerful theological vision. This problem is formed by what one might call the continual fluctuation between solitude and life in community, the oscillation and, finally, the combination and balance which are progressively established between these two elements.

*   *   *   *   *   *   *   *   *   *   *

From the very beginning of monastic history the problem had made itself acutely felt. It was to require the brilliant account, in the form of an apology by a bishop of Alexandria, St Athanasius in his *Life of Antony*, to give standing to the eremitical custom—up to that time considered strange, of separating oneself from the parish community in order to go and pitch one's tent in the wilderness. And all the author's theological skill would go into the business of proving how, through the crucible of solitude, Antony finally became invested with a universal fatherhood which made him still more available for all men, without endangering the strictest solitude possible, the *interiora deserti*, which he continued to love and seek above everything.

We might glean numerous traces of the same problem in the *Apophthegms*. The whole body of work attributed to St Arsenius, for example, aims to explain how he is thus able to be passionately desirous of solitude without however being deficient in charity. The problem is taken up again in all modes and tones. Even the intellectual Evagrius cannot escape it, although he is content to answer it with an aphorism, very much in his own manner, but one which opens up immense perspectives: 'The monk is one who is separated from all and united to all.'

John Cassian in his turn inherits the same problem and it pervades his *Conferences*. Fascinated by the ideal of extreme solitude of which he had encountered some outstanding examples in the course of his travels, Cassian nevertheless examines all its risks. He is in any case writing for coenobites, very few of whom would be called to such exploits. This no doubt explains that perpetual hesitation which seems to run through his account, so great is his delight in detailing the advantages as well as the dangers of both solutions alike. In most cases, however, the solution is not to choose one of the two forms of life to the exclusion of the other. It is rather to combine the advantages of both in the wisest possible manner so as to reduce the respective dangers of each. It is in this way that St Gregory of Nazianzus hails the monastic work of St Basil:

> As the eremitical life and the coenobitic life were becoming distinct from each other in several respects, and as neither the one nor the other possessed only advantages or only disadvantages, but the one, being more peaceful and quiet and more conducive to union with God, was more free from pride because there virtue was less subject to comparison, the other being more active and useful, but less free from clamour, Basil reconciled them perfectly together and combined them, establishing cells quite close to those who were living all together in community without, however, keeping the two apart as if by a wall built between them, but rather uniting them while at the same separating them, so that the contemplative life was not antagonistic to life in community,

nor the active life to contemplation, but in the same way as the earth and the sea, so these two lives, communicating to each other their mutual advantages, co-operated for the sole glory of God.[2]

The way in which this combination is worked out in practice can have any number of variations. But never, in one way or another, does the search for solitude entirely exclude a certain practical exercise of charity. There are those who put the emphasis on solitude, like the kind of life described by Rufinus of Aquileia in his *History of the Monks* (in words foreshadowing Peter Damian): 'They are scattered in the desert and in separate cells, but they are united in charity.' The motives advanced by Rufinus on behalf of this emphasis on solitude are already those of hesychasm: 'They live thus in separate dwelling-places so that, as they meditate on the things of God in the calm of silence and with attentive minds, no voice, no encounter, no idle discourse may disturb them.' They live together, but without any detriment to solitude: 'While forming a large multitude, they live as solitaries. Their whole manner of life is in the fact of being established in a group, as if they were living in the desert.'[3] On Sundays they meet together to celebrate as brothers the joy of the Resurrection.

At the other end of the scale, the balance extolled by Dorotheus of Gaza is more subtle and varied. According to him, appealing to the teaching of the ancient Fathers, 'to stay in one's cell is one half, and to go and see the Old Men is another half'. The atmosphere is at first, it seems, more coenobitic, although an important emphasis is still placed on the cell. Dorotheus endeavours to explain why the monk must also sometimes leave his cell to go and see other brothers. He sees three motives for this. The first is that of charity. Dorotheus is content to recall in this connection an ancient apophthegm, which was already to be found in the writings of Tertullian before it was heard in the saying of the ancient Fathers: 'When you see your brother you see the Lord your God.' The second motive seems to us today to be surprisingly modern. Dorotheus declares that it is easier to listen to the Word of God when several brothers meet to read it together. The third motive concerns spiritual discernment. Solitude can be a source of illusion. In this respect the encounter with the brothers plays the part of a revelatory test. It discloses to the solitary his true state, 'for the cell exalts, but men put to the test'. Often one comes out of these encounters mortified in some new way. But the gain is in depth, if the solitary is able to take advantage of it to grow in humility: 'He acknowledges his weakness and declares that he has so far learned nothing in solitude. He returns to his cell humiliated, he weeps, he does penance, he calls on God to help him in his weakness and remains thus watchful of himself.'[4]

Very soon in the East a particular type of life appears which St John Climacus extols as a middle way, or a royal way, between the stricter eremitism and coenobitism, that of the solitary life lived in small groups, gathered round a spiritual Father. The ideal, magnificently built up anew by St Nil Sorskij in sixteenth-century Russia, survives in Orthodoxy to this day.

* * * * * * * * * * * * *

The West has not remained ignorant of it, even if it has lived it on slightly different lines. In the West, too, hermits who are strictly and absolutely solitary have always been very rare. One who has an expert knowledge of western eremitism could write: 'One of the characteristics of the eremitism of the Middle Ages was that it was hardly ever individual.'[5] At the point of departure of the eremitical life, or at its point of arrival, almost always there appears a bond with one's brothers and with the Church, which tends to increase in importance. An attentive study of the documents concerning reclusion—that typically western form of the solitary life—would be sufficient, for example, to prove this. Grimlaic's *Regula solitariorum* is significant here. The recluse whom he is addressing is rarely alone, and the bonds which unite him to his companion or companions in reclusion may appear more severe than those which unite together the necessarily more numerous coenobites in a large monastery.[6]

A few centuries later *The Ancren Riwle* depicts a very similar situation in England. There are now three recluses living together, each in her own particular cell, of course, but each cell has three windows, one looking on to the church, another on to the neighbouring cell, and finally a third on to the outside world through which visitors are received and listened to. This community element in the life of the recluses seems moreover to have a certain weight since the author of the document makes a point of congratulating his correspondents on the great unity of mind and heart which reigns among them, and which makes them, in his opinion, the most peaceful group of recluses he knows in England among the twenty others with whom he is acquainted.

We must, however, go back still further in order to discover the beginnings, in the West, of this balance between the solitary life and brotherly intercourse. According to Eucherius of Lyons, it is to the ancient Fathers of Lérins that the West owes the practice, which he says is Egyptian, of living together, but in separate cells: *divisis cellulis Aegyptios Patres Gallis nostris intulerunt*—'those Fathers introduced into our country of Gaul the individual cells of Egypt.'[7] And yet the Lérins community does indeed retain the appearance of a Church, if one may say so, living this desert ideal in community. The same Eucherius also hails it as a *sanctorum coetus conventusque*—'a meeting and association of saints'. And Sidonius Apollinaris, in a letter to Faustus, a former monk of Lérins, recently raised to the episcopate, recalls the holy company of solitaries whom he has just left, with the names of *congregatio eremitis*—'group of hermits'—or *senatus Lirinensium cellulanorum*—'the council of cell-dwellers in Lérins'.[8] The abundance and precision of this vocabulary relating to community prove the extent to which shared solitude or, if you like, corporate solitude, already corresponded to a particular grace whose elements were correctly observed by contemporaries.

Much later the reforming movement of the eleventh and twelfth centuries brings a new emphasis on solitude into monastic experience. The twelfth century is marked, among other things, by a return to the desert. the *heremus*—desert—then becomes a sign and safeguard of authenticity. Yet it is a desert marked more than ever by the demands of brotherly love. Very often this powerful eremitical movement, born in the woods and marshes, shows a tendency to become organized in a ceonobitic life. By way of example, among several others, one may cite the monks of Obazine whom the Chronicle describes as *monachi ex eremitis effecti*—hermits who became monks.[9] But above all, this period sees the birth of several forms of eremitical life lived in community, some of which have continued in existence up to the present day.

In the twelfth century a canon regular, Raimbaud of Liége, tries to see clearly into this great ferment of tendencies and observances. Among the monks he distinguishes three families. The first live among men—*monachi qui iuxta homines habitant*. The Cluniacs are the supreme example of these. The second settle far from men—*monachi qui longe se ab hominibus faciunt*. One thinks of the Cistercians. Thirdly and finally, one considers the hermits who live alone or in small groups—*eremitae qui pauciores sunt et soli saepe habitant vil cum paucis*.[10] Even if they tend to live completely alone, brotherly intercourse is not excluded. Proof of this is found in the

Life of St Bernard of Tiron in which a description of the eremitical life on the borders of Brittany shows how the most secluded solitaries meet from time to time to confer together—*more concilii.*[11]

But at this point we should study particularly the original eremitical movement which, by way of charismatic masters like Romuald and Bruno and Stephen of Grandmont, resulted in the establishment of actual religious Orders whose chief grace consists in this delicate proportioning of the attraction for the solitary life and the attraction for life in community. To be sure, the way had been paved for their appearance. Dom Jean Leclercq has recalled that the lavra form of eremitism, still little studied today, must have been very widespread in the Italian peninsula during the early Middle Ages. There is an illustrious example of it in Monte Luco, not far from Spoleto, which has been called the 'Italian desert', and where lavra and coenobia stood side by side.[12] These preparations pass into the Romualdian movement.

Thanks to Peter Damian, we have a fairly good idea of St Romuald's intentions when he entered on his campaign to reform the eremitical life. St Romuald acknowledged that his personal grace had been perfectly stated in the *Liber de Vita Patrum.* This reference is important. It situates his work within the great tradition. It was from there that he drew the image of the eremitical life which he was henceforth to propagate. It is the picture, as St Peter Damian recalls, of brothers fasting in solitude for the whole week but meeting together on Saturdays and Sundays in order to enjoy some relaxation as brothers—*ut ieiunii rigorem interponerent et remissius victitarent.*[13] Romuald was henceforth to regard this rhythm of monastic life as the ideal one. He combines a distinct bias in favour of the solitary life with a cautious but positive advance towards life in community. He even attempts to impose this ideal on the abbots of large coenobitic monasteries whose reform he undertook, suggesting a week of silence in the cell, broken by a day given over to visiting and receiving one's brothers.[14] Wherever Romuald goes with his zeal for reform, he suggests the same balance. On the one hand he gathers the brothers together in obedience under a superior and a common rule; on the other he separates them each in his individual cell.[15]

Among the many foundations strewn along the whole length of the route travelled by St Romuald that of Camaldoli was destined to be particularly successful. What is probably the most ancient codification of the customs of the desert, which we owe to Blessed Rudolph of Camaldoli,[16] has preserved a fairly faithful picture of the normal rhythm of Romuald's monasteries. Alongside the recluses who leave their hermitages only very rarely, the other hermits go to the church for the celebration of the liturgy only on Sundays and twelve lesson feasts. On these same days they share a common refectory. A spiritual exhortation in chapter is restricted to important feasts only.

In the same period another foundation was seeking a similar balance: that achieved by St Bruno in the desert of the Grande Chartreuse. This foundation did indeed involve a real quest, and one which probably did not fail to arouse astonishment as well as wariness. In his *Golden Epistle*, addressed to the Carthusians of Mont-Dieu, William of St-Thierry assures them that the amazing Carthusian balance between solitude and community life has its roots in a very ancient tradition of the Church: '*Sed haec novitas non est novella vanitas. Res enim est antiquae religionis, perfectae fundatae in Christo pietatis, antiqua haereditas Ecclesiae*' (But this new custom is not a vain novelty. It is something founded on ancient religious practice, the perfection of that devotion which has Christ as its source, an inheritance from the early Church).[17] And he adds that this manner of life represents the light of the East coming, through the Carthusian customs, to dispel the darkness of the West.

In many respects, even including the ritual which solemnly installs the novice in his cell, Carthusian solitude, strictly confined within the area of the hermitage and its little garden, recalls that of the recluses. Except for the Offices in which, originally, he joined with the others only twice a day, the Carthusian rarely has a sufficient motive for emerging from his solitude. The celebration of the Mass, too, is fairly rare, for the concern for solitude and *quies* surpasses all others. On the other hand, Sundays and feast days are spent more or less as in coenobitic monasteries, and that materially small portion of life set aside for brotherly intercourse is always cultivated with great attention. These, for example, are the words in which Dom Innocent Le Masson, the Prior of the Grande Chartreuse in the seventeenth century, justifies the practice of weekly strolls or walks:

> There are proportions and bounds to be observed in solitude and silence in order to practise them all together and to bring them suitably within men's capacity, for no more than their bodies, can their minds adapt themselves to what is extreme. That is why it is very necessary to take care not to follow, in this matter, the speculations and imaginations of an excessive enthusiasm if one wants to avoid

becoming unable to use one's mind and one's body, and making oneself useless to the community and a burden to oneself. Experience has caused this truth to be clearly seen in the Carthusian Order, and that is the reason why it has changed all the Colloquies, which in former times used to be addressed to the community, into a walk—called a *Spatiament*—which takes place each week and from which no one of our brothers is granted exemption. Nor do we allow anyone to absent himself from it without a very legitimate reason, and one that requires the permission of the Superior, because we consider this walk as an observance and a means which helps us to put all others into practice.[18]

At the Grande Chartreuse another mode of brotherly intercourse appears from the beginning: the desire to have a further influence other than by prayer alone, by a visible activity, but one which is in no way harmful to solitude: the transcription of manuscripts. Another Carthusian author, Adam Scot, hails this work as a speciality of the eremitical life, an immortal work in the service of the spiritual benefit of all.[19]

All these community customs, even when they become quite visible, yet remain entirely at the service of the solitary, that is, the *hidden* life. That point must be insisted upon. Perhaps the most striking example of this is seen in the actual person of the superior of this little eremitical fraternity. By his office he is entirely at the service of the common good of the group. He must, however, before all else be a living example of all the virtues proper to the eremitical state, virtues which he must show forth in himself—*sculpta per expressionem sanctitatis*.[20] For Blessed Rudolph of Camaldoli, quoted earlier, this list of eremitical virtues is long and impressive. The Prior of the Grande Chartreuse, Blessed Guiguo, who codified Bruno's customs in the *Consuetudines Carthusiae*, is more restrained but no less incisive. On the subject of the prior he recalls the essential thing: he must be an example of peace and solitariness to all—*quietis et solitudinis exemplum omnibus det*. This example was so exacting that Guiguo requires the Prior of the Grande Chartreuse never to go beyond the confines of the desert for any reason whatsoever. Thus the one who is the symbol and the very centre of life in a brotherhood, the prior of the eremitical community, also becomes, as it were, the sign and sacrament of seclusion.

We may point out here that Stephen of Grandmont requires a similar example from the superior of his foundation:

Your superior must be careful in every way never to leave the enclosure of Grandmont unless forced to do so by essential business. Let him realise clearly that as long as he is bound by the chains of Christ, he must refuse to go into the world, lest any of his followers should dare to disobey him . . . for the same Lord who holds the superior captive by his love, also holds captive the disciples.[21]

* * * * * * * * * *

BEFORE concluding these brief investigations, it is fitting to point out another milieu, this time coenobitic, in which we meet about the same period a similar concern to attain a certain balance between the values of solitude and those of brotherly intercourse. I am referring to the Cistercians of the twelfth century who were very strongly characterised, it seems, by the desert places in which they went to settle. The concern for this balance is expressed in almost the same vocabulary as that used by the hermits living in lavras. In order to be persuaded of this, it will be sufficient to place two texts side by side. In the first a Carthusian, in his *Life of St Hugh of Lincoln*, describes the balance attained by the Carthusian life. In the second we shall hear William of St-Thierry describe a very similar balance in the experience of the Cistercians of Clairvaux.

This is how the young Hugh of Lincoln makes his first encounter with the Grande Chartreuse. The image which struck him, and which was to be the origin of his vocation, admirably mingles the two aspects, that of solitude and that of intercourse:

Their statutes recommended, not singleness, but solitude. Their cells are separated, but their hearts are united. Each one lives apart, but no one possesses anything apart. All live alone, and yet each one acts with the community. One is alone and one thus avoids the disadvantages of society, but one lives sufficiently in common not to be deprived of the consolation afforded by the company of one's brothers. All this delighted St Hugh and he desired at all costs to embrace this Carthusian life.[22]

And now see how William of St-Thierry discovers a similar combination of the two aspects in the Cistercian life, which is yet to all intents and purposes so different from Carthusian solitude:

All in the solitude of that place, with dense forests surrounded by

26

mountains, were solitaries, in spite of their great number. A well-regulated charity made this valley, which was full of men, solitary for each one of them. Thanks to unity of spirit and the observance of the silence, the Order safeguarded solitude of heart for each member of that ordered multitude.[23]

Cîteaux, in the twelfth century, had indeed this common life, though lived in the desert, and thanks to the strictness of the life, it restored and made possible an authentic eremitical and hesychastic experience. See, moreover, how another Cistercian, Guerric of Igny, discovers and describes the same balance:

> By a wonderful grace it is given to us to enjoy in our deserts the calm of solitude, without being deprived of the consolation of holy society. Each one can be at peace, solitary, in silence, for no one addresses him. And yet he does not draw down upon himself the curse pronounced against the man who is alone and has no one to support him. He has no fear of being alone, deprived of the friendship that would cheer him, or the hand that would lift him up if he were to fall. We are here in the company of men, and yet away from the crowd. In our wilderness we combine the calm of solitude with the comfort of holy society. We live as in a town, and yet no clamour prevents us from hearing the voice of him who cries in the wilderness, only provided that our inner silence corresponds to this outward silence.[24]

The striking parallelism between these two spiritualities, the Carthusian and the Cistercian, both of them at the same time eremitical and fraternal, and yet so different from each other as regards the outward manner of life, is a new proof of what these few lines are trying to show: that the other, hidden, evangelical, side of all solitude eventually discloses itself as a life lived in common in one way or another; and that the other, hidden, evangelical, side of all true community life is solitude in God and for his sake, towards whom it must always lead.

Our conclusion can be brief. From whatever side one looks at it, Christian solitude passes into fulness of communion; it is always corporate—*solitudo pluralis*. The cell, in the words of St Peter Damian, is '*conclave sanctae Ecclesiae*'—the meeting-place of Holy Church.[25] One perseveres in it, not for oneself, but in the service of all: '*Magna tamen est sapientia, magnaque misericordia, dum in secreto Dei possunt quiescere, ut ibi maneant ad communem omnuim utilitatem.*' (There is great wisdom and great mercy in remaining peacefully in secret with God, for those who stay there do so for the good of all.)[26]

And the consummation of solitude, its ripe fruit, is the sweetness of love, that with which God has filled the solitary, and which now, through him, is available for all men. The true solitary finally appears as gentle among the gentle. He radiates *pietas*, the tenderness which Blessed Rudolph of Camaldoli recommends as an indispensable eremitical virtue, that 'loving-kindness which comes out to meet disease and weakness with mercy and humanity'.[27] It matches the gratuitousness of love, extolled by Blessed Guiguo, which has no other *raison d'être* than its own sweetness: '*Optanda est dilectio gratis, id est propter suam dulcedinem propriam, tamquam nectar suavissimum*', which is to say: Best of all is the grace of love, which enjoys its own sweetness—the sweetest honey of all.[28]

NOTES

1. *PL* 145, col. 231 ff. esp. nos. 5-10. For an English trans. see P. McNulty, op. cit. n. 1 of A. M. Allchin's article.

2. *PG* 36, Gregory of Nazianzen, *Oratio 43, In Laudem Basilii Magni*, col. 578.

3. *PL* 21, cols. 389 ff.

4. Dorotheus of Gaza, *Oeuvres Spirituelles*, ed. and trans. (French) L. Regnault J. de Préville, *Sources Chrétiennes* 92, (Paris, 1963) pp. 488-490.

5. J. de Trévillers, *Sequania monastica*, Vesoul (1955), vol. 2, 101.

6. *PL* 103, col. 573.

7. *PL* 58, *De Laudi Eremi*, col. 710.

8. *PL* 58, Letter 9, col. 618.

9. Ref. untraced. [Ed.]

10. *PL* 213, col. 814 ff.

11. *PL* 172, col. 1318.

12. Jean Leclercq, *L'érémitisme en Occident jusqu' à l'an mil* in *Le millénaire du Mont-Athos, 963-1963*, vol. I, 161-180.

13. *PL 144, Vita S. Romualdi*, 8, col. 962.

14. Ibid. 30 and 45.

15. Ibid. no. 26: *multis fratribus aggregatis*; no. 34: *ut communia cuncta facerent*; no. 26: *[his] per cellas singulas constitutis*.

16. *Regula eremitica*, edited in the *Annales Camaldulenses*, vol. III, pp. 512-43. The *Decretum generale de stabilitate vitae eremiticae* seems to reflect an earlier state of affairs than that known by the *Regula eremitica*.

17. *PL* 184, col. 310.

18. Interpretation of some passages in the ancient Statutes of the Carthusian Order (anonymous), *La Correrie* 1689. In fact the work, unofficial and addressed confidentially only to the priors of the Order, is a reply by the Prior of the Grande Chartreuse to a pamphlet whose author is the Abbé de Rancé.

19. *PL* 153, *De quadripertito exercitio cellae*, cols. 881 ff.; cf. *Consuetudines Guigonis*, ibid. col. 694.

20. *Regula eremitica*, 52 (see n. 16).

21. *PL* 204, *Regula* 62, col. 1160.

22. *PL* 153, *Vita S. Hugonis*, cap. 1, vi, cols. 951-2.

23. *PL* 185, *Vita Prima S. Bernardi*, i, 35, col. 248.

24. *PL* 185, Sermon for Advent IV, cols. 22-23. [For an English translation see Guerric of Igny, *Liturgical Sermons*, Vol. I, trans. Monks of Mount St Bernard Abbey, Cistercian Fathers Series (Irish University Press 1971), pp. 23 f.

25. *PL* 145, *De contemptu saeculi*, col. 275.

26. *PL* 204, *Regula* 54, col. 1156.

27. *Regula eremitica*, 42 (see n. 16).

28. *PL* 153, *Meditationes*, col. 626.

'SEPARATED FROM ALL AND UNITED TO ALL':

The Hermit Life in the Christian East

ARCHIMANDRITE KALLISTOS WARE

THE THREE WAYS

'The body is one and yet has many limbs, and all these limbs, though many, form a single body.' (I Cor. 12:12.) The analogy which St Paul applies here to the life of the Church as a whole can also be applied more specifically to the monastic vocation within the Church. All monks and nuns share the same ascetic call and belong to a single, all-embracing 'order' or 'estate'; yet within that one 'estate' there is a wide variety of patterns and a constant flexibility. This variety and flexibility must always be kept in view when considering the position, within the Orthodox monastic framework, of the hermit—of the one who, according to a famous definition by Evagrius of Pontus (d. 399), is 'separated from all and united to all'.[1]

The wide variety of patterns is reduced by St John Climacus (d. *circa* 649) to three main types. 'The monastic way of life', he says, 'takes three general forms: either to live in ascetic withdrawal and solitude, or to be a hesychast with one or two companions, or to dwell with patient endurance in a coenobium.'[2] These three forms—the coenobitic, the eremitic, and the middle or semi-eremitic way of the hesychast who dwells with one or two others—are found at the very outset of Christian monasticism in fourth-century Egypt. St Antony provided in his own person a living icon of the hermit ideal; St Pachomius established the coenobitic pattern; St Ammon at Nitria and St Macarius at Scetis mapped out the intermediate path. The same three forms can be found, sixteen centuries later, side by side in contemporary Athos. The twenty ruling monasteries exemplify the coenobitic discipline, although in some houses the full strictness of this has been modified by the introduction of the idiorrhythmic system.[3] The semi-eremitic way (it could with equal appropriateness be styled 'semi-coenobitic') is found in the little monastic cottages known as 'kalyvai' or 'kellia', with between two and six brethren, or very occasionally with more than six. In some parts of Athos these kellia stand isolated, while elsewhere they are grouped in monastic villages called 'sketes', as at Great St Anne's or Kapsokalyvia. Finally there are the hermits, a few of them closely dependent on a monastery, others loosely grouped together in what resembles a skete (as at Karoulia), others again living in extreme seclusion, almost entirely hidden, with the path to their cell known perhaps to none save the priest who brings them communion.

The coexistence of these three forms of the monastic life means that there is more than one way in which a man may prepare to be a hermit. At least three doors of entry into solitude are found in the practice of contemporary Athos. A monk, after living for some years in a monastery, may go with the abbot's blessing to a kellion, there to follow the semi-eremitic life; and after that he may withdraw into the life of fully eremitic solitude. In such a case he experiences in succession each of the three main forms of the monastic life. This we may call the 'classic pattern' of preparation. But there are two other possibilities. A monk may go out from the coenobium to become a hermit, without first living in a semi-eremitic kellion; or he may at the outset enter a semi-eremitic kellion and so become a hermit, without ever having lived in a coenobium. This last course is by far the most usual way of becoming a hermit on Athos today.

When a man goes directly from the monastery to a hermit's cell, it is probable that he will maintain some continuing link with his previous community. He may return there regularly for the Liturgy; the monastery may provide his basic food supplies; he may even be recalled by the community to live again, temporarily or permanently, within the monastery walls. The hermit who has lived previously in a skete or an isolated kellion is in a different situation. It is true that he is theoretically dependent on a monastery, since the entire territory of Athos is divided between the twenty ruling monasteries, with the result that every semi-eremitic kellion and every hermit is in principle subject to one of these twenty ruling houses. But in practice the bond is not likely to be close. The hermit may of course choose to visit the monastery to attend services, especially at great feasts, but the monastic community is not under any obligation to support him (although in fact it often gives him food), and it cannot require him against his will to move into the monastery.

Between the hermit and the monk in a coenobium there is a plain and manifest distinction. But the line of demarcation is far less sharply drawn

C

between the hermit and the monk following the semi-eremitic way in a kellion. The kelliot may for example find himself left alone through the death of his companions, and so may become *de facto* a solitary, without any deliberate decision on his part. Again, a man who has lived for some years as a hermit may then be joined by disciples; and so, imperceptibly, he moves from the solitary to the middle or semi-eremitic state. Such transitions are easily made in the sketes of contemporary Athos. The degree of physical isolation varies greatly in the case of individual hermits; as already emphasized, flexibility is the norm. Some hermits live close to their neighbours and meet them daily; others, because of distance or from personal choice, have virtually no contact with their fellows. There are even solitaries on Athos today who follow the same way of life as the *boskoi* in primitive monasticism—dwelling with the animals like Adam in Paradise, not building cells but remaining in caves or in the open air, wearing no clothing and eating no cooked food. Although I have not myself seen any such, I have spoken with monks who know about them.[4]

Such, in broad outline, is the situation of the hermit in Eastern monasticism. Let us give detail to this picture by reviewing some of the historical evidence.

FOURTH-CENTURY EGYPT

Two points strike us at the outset. First, there was initially a clear separation between the coenobitic and the eremitic vocations: in fourth-century Egypt it was not the Pachomian coenobia but the semi-eremitic centres such as Nitria that served as a training-ground for hermits. Secondly, in the formation of the hermit, from the start primary importance was attached to the need for personal spiritual direction under an 'abba' or 'elder'—what the Greek sources call a *gerōn* and what the Russians were later to term a *starets*. The variety and flexibility of Eastern monasticism must inevitably seem ill-disciplined and untidy to the Western mind, unless it is remembered that underlying this variety there is the direct personal relationship between the spiritual father and his child. This relationship, while it ensures inner order within seeming confusion, is not something that can be contained within institutional forms or controlled by rules.

The importance of spiritual fatherhood is seen at the very beginning of monastic history in the life of St Antony. When he first hears the call to sell everything and to take up the cross, he does not withdraw at once into the desert but seeks out in the next village an old man who is experienced in the ascetic way and whom he can take as his model.[5] Only some fifteen years later does Antony go out into the further desert and dwell entirely on his own, with none to guide him; and even then he tries to persuade the old man to accompany him.[6] Thus even the pioneer Antony, before becoming a solitary, learnt obedience under others. The significance attached to obedience by Antony—or at any rate by the early monastic tradition—is evident from two 'words' attributed to him in *The Sayings of the Desert Fathers*:

> I know of monks who fell away after many labours and lapsed into madness, because they put their trust in their own work and despised the commandment that says, 'Ask your father and he will tell you.' (Deut. 32:7.)

> If possible, a monk ought to tell the elders how many steps he takes and how many drops of water he drinks in his cell, in case he is in error about it.[7]

In the earliest monasticism, then, the aspiring hermit is tested and trained under the personal care of an abba, and not by the observance of the rule in a coenobium. The kind of formation that an abba imparts is indicated in the story told by Palladius about St Antony and Paul the Simple.[8] Even if the details here are not historically true of Antony himself, the account illustrates how the preparation for the hermit life was envisaged in Egypt at the end of the fourth century. Paul journeys from his village to Antony's cell in the desert and knocks on the door, asking to become a monk. Antony tells him that he is too old to embark on the hardships of the solitary life; let him go to a coenobium. Paul refuses to go away. After leaving him for a long time on the doorstep, Antony becomes afraid that Paul will die there, and so reluctantly he takes him into his cell. The training is very simple: without giving any theoretical teaching, Antony keeps Paul with him in his cell and tells him what tasks he must perform. They work, pray and eat together. Paul does exactly as he is told, without asking any questions. Then, 'after the required number of months' (we are not told how many), Antony says to Paul: 'See, you have become a monk; go and live on your own, so as to gain experience of the demons.' He then settles Paul in a cell some four miles away. Presumably Antony continues to give him some kind of guidance, but they no longer live together. In this way, after the training of shared life in a kellion, Paul is allowed to become

33

a solitary.

St Pachomius begins in the same way as St Antony. On receiving the call to become a monk, his first action is to seek out an 'old man', the hermit Palamon, under whose direction he learns the ascetic way.[9] Pachomius' subsequent path diverges from Antony's, for after an initial period as a hermit he founds a coenobium. There is, however, no reason to believe that he was opposed to the hermit life on principle. He envisaged the coenobitic form of monasticism, not necessarily as superior to the anachoretic form, but simply as different. In his eyes the coenobitic and eremitic vocations were mutually exclusive alternatives; the coenobium was not a training-ground for hermits but something complete in itself to which a man was committed permanently until death.

Thus a young man in the middle of the fourth century, feeling the call of the solitary life, would not have turned to a Pachomian house. He would have gone rather to a semi-eremitic centre such as Nitria, which from the start was orientated towards the eremitic ideal. With its central church and guest house and its scattered monastic cottages, Nitria must have resembled a skete in contemporary Athos, apart from the fact that Nitria was much larger. The aspirant, on arrival at Nitria, entered one of the kellia in the central part of the settlement; here he shared a common life with others, learning monastic obedience under a spiritual father. After a time he might move to the more remote area of the Cells and there live as a solitary. Between Nitria and the Cells there was no sharp boundary; the solitaries lived on the margin of the semi-eremitic settlements, and though secluded they were still an integral part of the total community of Nitria. No precise period of preparation was laid down before the move to the Cells could take place. Evagrius spent two years at Nitria before moving out to the Cells; Palladius spent two years at Nitria before he withdrew there.[10] But both had some experience of the monastic life before coming to Nitria; otherwise the time of preparation might well have been more prolonged.

Texts such as *The Sayings of the Desert Fathers* or the writings of Evagrius, which reflect the Nitrian tradition, continually insist that, without rigorous training under a spiritual father in the shared life of the kellion, no one should attempt to live in solitude. 'If you have not first of all lived rightly with men,' stated Abba Lucius, 'you will not be able to live rightly in solitude.'[11] Elsewhere the *Sayings of the Desert Fathers* tell of a young monk who, as soon as he was given the habit, shut himself in his cell as a recluse. The elders came and smashed down the enclosure, forcibly ejecting him; and he was made to go round to all the brethren, saying: 'Forgive me, for I am not an anchorite but a beginner.'[12] In one text it is even suggested that communal life under an abba is higher than the eremitic vocation because of the opportunity it provides to practise obedience: 'One who lives in submission under a spiritual father has a greater reward than one who withdraws by himself into the desert.'[13] But generally in the *Sayings of the Desert Fathers* there is a reluctance to make direct comparisons. When asked which way of life is the better, Patriarch Cyril of Alexandria wisely replied: 'It is impossible to choose between Elijah and Moses, for they both pleased God.'[14]

While the hermit ideal is greatly admired in the Nitrian sources its dangers are not forgotten. The most serious of these is exposure to demonic attacks. As we have seen, when Antony sent Paul to a cell on his own, this was precisely that he might 'gain experience of the demons'. The solitary has to encounter Satan directly, face to face, in a way that the coenobite usually does not. When a monk lives with others, states Evagrius,[15] the demons attack him indirectly, through the annoyances caused to him by his brethren and through the varying tensions of the communal life; but when he goes out into the desert, the demons no longer use men as intermediary but attack directly. However trying our brethren may be, it is incomparably easier to put up with them than to meet the demons. And just as demons are more terrible than men, so the solitary life is much harder than the communal. St Seraphim of Sarov (1759-1833), who knew at first hand the life of both coenobite and hermit, had no illusions which was the more exacting: 'He was reluctant to advise others to live in the desert. One who lives in the desert, he warned, must be like a man nailed to the cross; and he added that if, in the struggle against the enemy, monks in a monastery fought as though they contended with doves, the man in the desert had to fight as one contending with lions and tigers.'[16] In the words of another Russian, St Nil Sorsky (d. 1508), 'Solitude demands the fortitude of an angel.'[17]

BASIL, CASSIAN AND BENEDICT

St Basil of Caesarea, who along with St Pachomius is the chief pioneer of the coenobitic ideal in the Christian East, seems to go beyond Pachomius in voicing open reservations about the eremitic way. 'Who does not know', he protests, 'that man is a tame and sociable animal, not solitary and wild?

For nothing is so characteristic of our nature as to associate with one another, to need one another, and to love our own kind.'[18] The solitary lacks the opportunity to show practical compassion towards others, and to manifest obedience and humility: 'Whose feet will you wash, whom will you look after, how can you be last of all, if you live by yourself?'[19] But Basil's hostility to the hermit life should not be exaggerated. In his early days he had himself lived in seclusion, with his friend St Gregory of Nazianzus; and if in later years as a bishop he sought to foster a monasticism closely integrated into the life of the Church as a whole, such as he had seen in Syria, this did not imply a total rejection of the solitary way. In a letter to his disciple Chilo, he stresses the difficulties of the hermit life but admits the validity of the hermit vocation.[20] Gregory of Nazianzus said that Basil sought to reconcile and unite the solitary and the common life by founding cells for anchorites not far from his coenobitic houses.[21]

Here, possibly, we can see emerging the idea, absent from Pachomian monasticism, that the coenobium may act as a nursery for anchorites, although certainly St Basil did not envisage that as its primary purpose. This idea of the coenobium as a first stage, leading on to the life of solitude, is much more explicit in St John Cassian. He speaks of the *prima scola coenobii* from which the monk can then advance to the *secundus anachoreseos gradus.*[22] But at the same time he enlarges upon the extreme perils of living in solitude, exposed to savage attacks from the demons;[23] here he is of course reproducing the teaching of his master Evagrius. Only the perfect, he says, should withdraw alone into the desert[24] —and who dare call himself perfect? He commends such figures as Paphnutius, who attained sanctity while still in a coenobium,[25] and John, who found himself unequal to the hermit life and so returned to the community.[26] Thus, while upholding the solitary life as an ultimate goal, he evidently considers that the great majority of monks will remain for all their lives in the community. The general tendency of his writings is to discourage rather than to propagate the hermit vocation. Cassian himself had dwelt initially in a coenobium at Bethlehem before living in the semi-eremitic milieu of Nitria and in the deeper seclusion of Scetis and the Cells. It is significant that on settling in Gaul he founded coenobia, not sketes, for training hermits.

St Benedict of Nursia's attitude is close to that of Cassian, but carries somewhat further the emphasis upon the coenobitic life as the general norm for monasticism. Like Pachomius, Benedict began as a hermit, and he nowhere attacks the hermit ideal as such, but only its abuses. His phrase *minima inchoationis regula*[27] recalls Cassian's remark about the *prima scola*. Perhaps, then, Benedict thought that his monks, after being trained by his *Rule* in the rudiments of monasticism, might then go on to be solitaries. But he nowhere specifies precisely what steps a monk would take in such a case. In the Benedictine, as in the Pachomian Rule, the coenobium is treated as a self-contained whole. This failure to provide practical directions on how to become a hermit, together with the heavy stress on the virtue of stability, inevitably tended to discourage men from becoming solitaries.

THE PALESTINIAN PATTERN

To find the coenobium treated, in a fully developed and explicit way, as a preparation for solitude, we must turn from Pachomius, Basil and Benedict to the monastic centres founded in the Judaean wilderness by St Euthymius (d. 473) and his disciple St Sabas (d. 532). They established a three-tier system, which we have described above as the 'classic pattern'. The postulant was expected to go first to the coenobium to receive his monastic formation. From there he might be allowed, after some years of preliminary training, to advance to a lavra: this was a form of the semi-eremitic way, usually with the monks living each in a separate cave, yet remaining in fairly close proximity to one another and meeting for common worship on Saturdays and Sundays. A few monks might eventually move from the lavra into yet greater seclusion, becoming hermits in the full sense.

This 'classic pattern' is exemplified in St Sabas' own life. When he first sought admission to the lavra of St Euthymius as a young man aged eighteen, Euthymius would not allow him to remain there but sent him to the nearby coenobium of Theoctistus. 'My child', says Euthymius, 'it is not right for you to stay in a lavra, for you are still young; it is better for the young in a coenobium.'[28] After twelve years of coenobitic life, Sabas was allowed to move to a cave near the monastery; here he existed in a semi-eremitic situation, spending five days of each week in solitude within his cave, and returning to his monastery for Saturday and Sunday. Then, after five more years, he withdrew into the utter desert, meeting no one and living on wild plants. Thus he passed through all three forms of monastic life before himself becoming an abbot and spiritual father. In his turn he imposed on others the same pattern as Euthymius had imposed on him. Young applicants were not admitted immediately to the lavra but sent to a special coenobium established for novices; after being tested in the common life they might then be allowed to have a cell on their own in the lavra.[29] Sabas tells John the Hesychast: 'Just as the blossom precedes the fruit, the coenobitic life precedes the anachoretic.'[30]

Here then, in the Palestinian foundations of St Euthymius and St Sabas, we see the Eastern monastic pattern in its fully evolved form, as perpetuated in our own day upon Mount Athos. But in practice many other variations have continued to exist. In Gaza, for example, at the beginning of the sixth century there is the coenobium under Abbot Seridos, and living on the edge of this are two 'old men', hermits in strict enclosure, St Varsanuphius the Great and St John the Prophet. The two solitaries act as spiritual guides to the brethren of the coenobium, including the Abbot, as well as to many outside people.[31] In this case, then, we have hermits and a coenobium, but not the intermediate stage of the lavra or skete. The notion that one or more hermits, and not the abbot, should be spiritual guides for a coenobium, is perhaps surprising by Benedictine standards, but it is by no means unusual in the Christian East. On contemporary Athos, for example, close to the monastery of Stavronikita, there lives as a hermit the lay monk Paisios, who acts as spiritual father to the abbot, Archimandrite Basil (a priest), and to the rest of the brethren.

CANONICAL LEGISLATION

The main ruling on the eremitic life in Orthodox canon law (Canon 41 of the Council *in Trullo*, A.D. 692), speaks of hermits in relation to the coenobium, but says nothing about the intermediate or semi-eremitic state:

> Those who wish to withdraw into enclosure either in towns or in villages, and to be attentive to themselves in solitude, must first enter a monastery and there be trained in the manner of life appropriate to a hermit. For a period of three years they must with fear of God be subject to the superior of the house, showing due obedience in everything, and thus making it plain that their choice of the eremitic life is voluntary and whole-hearted. They are then to be examined by the local bishop; and after that they are to continue for one more year outside enclosure, so that the stability of their intention can be further tested. They are to provide clear evidence that they choose the life of stillness, not from any desire for empty glory, but because of its intrinsic value. When these four years have

38

elapsed, if they persist in their intention they are then to be enclosed. Thereafter they shall not be allowed to leave their seclusion whenever they wish, unless it be for the common benefit or because they are forced to do so by some compelling reason endangering their life; and even then they shall first obtain the blessing of the local bishop.[32]

Anyone familiar with the Orthodox attitude towards canon law will not be surprised to learn that these conditions are widely disregarded. The basic principle underlying the Canon, that the hermit must first have some experience of monastic life shared with others and pursued under obedience, is of course generally accepted. But the Canon goes beyond this in specifying detailed conditions:

(i) The prospective hermit is to spend at least three years in a coenobium under obedience to the abbot.
(ii) He will then be examined by the diocesan bishop; after that, on completing a further preparatory year, he may be permitted to enter solitude.
(iii) He can leave his seclusion only for grave reasons and with the bishop's blessing.

In laying down these conditions, the Canon seems to have primarily in mind one particular type of hermit, the solitary strictly enclosed within his cell, most probably inside the monastery itself. The Byzantine commentators, however, give the Canon a wider application, taking it to refer broadly to all hermits and hesychasts. In practice its conditions have been modified in four main ways:

First, most of the larger Eastern monasteries are 'stavropegiac', that is, exempt from the jurisdiction of the diocesan bishop. Where this is the case, the decision to permit a monk to become a hermit rests with the abbot, usually acting in consultation with the monastic council of senior monks; the local bishop is not involved.

Secondly, the requirement of four years in community is on the whole regarded as a minimum. In most instances a far longer preparation would be expected. St Seraphim, for example, became a novice in 1778 and was professed in 1786, but it was not until 1794—sixteen years after his first entry to the community—that he was given the blessing to withdraw as a solitary into the forest, four miles from the monastic buildings.

Thirdly, the act of eremitic withdrawal is in practice far less irrevocable than Canon 41 of the Council *in Trullo* suggests. It is not uncommon for monks, after living for a time in solitude, to seek readmittance to the coenobium, even though there is no 'compelling reason endangering their life'; such a request would normally be granted without great difficulty. In becoming a hermit, a monk has not thereby severed all links with his community or forfeited the right to live there again. The abbot may himself order the hermit to return to the community, regardless of the latter's own preference. That was what happened to St Seraphim: after sixteen years in his forest retreat, his legs began to swell and he found it increasingly difficult to walk to the monastery for the Liturgy and Holy Communion. So in 1810 he was ordered by the abbot to leave his hermitage and return to the main community. (But he was then allowed to live strictly enclosed in a cell; he did not attend the services in the main church, but Communion was brought to him each Sunday in his cell.)

Fourthly, and most fundamentally, nothing is said in this Canon about the skete system, which is the normal door of entry to the eremitic life. Broadly interpreted, the Canon could be taken to mean that no one should settle in a skete without first living in a coenobium; and this, as we have seen, was the rule followed by St Euthymius and St Sabas. But in practice, at any rate on Athos, many monks go to live in sketes without any preliminary preparation in a coenobium, and this has been the case for centuries.

Contrary, therefore, to what is laid down in Canon 41 of the Council *in Trullo*, a man can become a hermit without any period of initial training in a coenobitic house.

ATHOS AND PATMOS

The foundation charters (*typika*) for two of the most celebrated coenobia in the Byzantine world—the Great Lavra on Athos and the monastery of St John the Theologian on Patmos (now, alas, both idiorrhythmic)—are noteworthy because of the relatively close link which they envisage between the hermits and the main coenobium.[33] Like Canon 41 of the Council *in Trullo*, these *typika* do not speak of the intermediate or skete way of life. Before the foundation of the Great Lavra in 963 by St Athanasius of Athos, there were on the Holy Mountain no coenobia but only hermits and isolated kellia, loosely federated under the elected leadership of a monk bearing the title *protos* and governed by periodical general assemblies at the monastic capital of Karyes. Since this loose federation had left room for confusion and disorder, Athanasius sought in his regulations for the Great Lavra to impose a fairly strict discipline over the hermits in the region of the monastery. He specifies that, among the 120 monks comprising the community of the Great Lavra, there should be not more than five solitaries, known as kelliots. These are to live outside the monastery, receiving food from the main community; each of them may have one disciple living with him, which means that their solitude was not necessarily to be total. These kelliots owe obedience to the abbot, and are definitely regarded as continuing to be members of the monastic brotherhood of the Great Lavra. Athanasius also states that a monk, with the abbot's blessing, may live enclosed as a solitary within his own cell inside the monastery walls.

In the foundation documents for the community of St John on Patmos, established by St Christodoulos in 1088, it is laid down that there may be at any one time not more than twelve solitaries living outside the main monastery and dependent upon it. Their continuing bond with the coenobium is underlined. They are to return each Saturday to the monastery, remaining for the vigil service that night, attending the Sunday morning Liturgy, and then going back to their hermitages on Sunday afternoon with sufficient food to last them through the week. They are also to come to the monastery on major feasts. While in the monastery the solitaries are to eat at the common table, but to speak with no one except the abbot. Equally they are not to speak with others while at their hermitages in the week. When in solitude during the week, they are to have one meal a day, after None, and are to eat only uncooked food. The solitaries remain under strict obedience to the abbot; if they show signs of self-will and insubordination, they will be at once recalled to live inside the monastery.

At the Great Lavra and St John's, Patmos, during more recent centuries, these rulings concerning hermits have undergone some modifications. The limitation in numbers envisaged by St Athanasius has long been disregarded. Thus in 1971 there were 50 monks living within the Great Lavra itself, but in the territory subject to it there were no less than 328 further monks: 156 living in sketes and 172 in isolated kellia.[34] Of these 328 monks, few if any were directly linked with the Great Lavra in the manner specified by the founder; the rest were virtually independent, each kelliot owing obedience to his own *geròn* rather than to the authorities in the main monastery.

On the island of Patmos at present there are a number of hermitages subject to the main monastery. All of these are now unoccupied except one where there is a single monk. He spends one week in every five at the main monastery, sharing in the work of the community and talking with the other monks in the normal way; otherwise he remains at his hermitage, attending the Sunday Liturgy at the nearest parish church. In the eighteenth and nineteenth centuries the hermitages each contained some two to four monks, living a semi-eremitic life. There were also hermits in the full sense: one still remembered on the island is the monk Theoktistos, who died at an advanced age in 1917 after spending part of his life on a waterless rock in the sea not far from Patmos, and part in a cave which he shared with a colony of adders.[35] These monks living in hermitages or as solitaries remained under obedience to the monastic authorities, but the rule that they should return to the main monastery each Saturday had long since fallen into disuse.

THE DAILY PROGRAMME OF A HERMIT

St Christodoulos, as we noted, expected his hermits to live, except at weekends, on uncooked vegetables and to eat only once a day, in the afternoon. A somewhat fuller description of a hermit's daily programme and diet is provided by St Gregory of Sinai (d.1346).[36] He divides the day into four periods of three hours each. Starting at dawn, the hesychast spends the first hour of the day on what Gregory terms 'quiet of the heart', the 'remembrance of God', and 'prayer'—that is, primarily the Jesus Prayer. The second hour is given to reading, and the third to *psalmōdia* or the recitation of the Psalter, which the hesychast would be expected to know by heart. The second and the third of the three-hour periods are devoted to the same three activities, in the same order. Then during the tenth hour of the day the hesychast prepares and eats his meal; during the eleventh, if he wishes, he may take a short rest; during the twelfth he recites Vespers. Presumably Terce, Sext and None, each taking about ten minutes, are said during the three periods assigned to psalmody, while Compline would have been said at sunset, shortly after Vespers.

For the night St Gregory proposes three alternative programmes. 'Beginners' are to spend half the night awake and half asleep, with midnight forming the point of division; it does not matter which half of the night is used for vigil. 'Intermediaries' (*mesoi*) are to spend the first two hours of the night awake, the next four asleep, and the remaining six awake. The 'perfect', who have no need of sleep, are to spend the whole night in vigil! During the waking hours of the night the hesychast recites the Midnight Office, Matins and Prime, devoting any time left over to the Jesus Prayer.

It is significant that the hermit is not exempted from reciting the Divine Office. St Gregory does not specify what is to happen if the hesychast cannot read; in that case, the Office was doubtless replaced by the Jesus Prayer, and in fact precise rules exist determining how this is to be done.[37] As in the regulations for Patmos, the hermit is to eat only once a day, after None and before Vespers. Gregory prescribes a basic diet of bread and water (mixed with a little wine), supplemented by fresh vegetables when available.[38] In Lent, probably the hermit did not eat until after Vespers; in the first week of Lent and during Holy Week, like many monks in the coenobia, he would doubtless try to observe so far as possible a total fast.

Surprisingly, St Gregory says nothing about manual labour. Presumably he expected the hesychast to practise some very simple handiwork such as basket-making, during which he could continue to recite the Psalms or the Jesus Prayer. (But St Gregory also expects the hesychast to devote certain periods of the day to saying the Jesus Prayer with undivided attention and unaccompanied by any manual work.) On Athos today most hermits cultivate little gardens; some pursue a handicraft such as icon-painting, wood-carving or the making of incense. Athonite solitaries, while they may receive bread from a monastery or nearby kellion, are on the whole expected to be self-supporting. The hermit applies to himself St Paul's words: 'These hands have ministered to my necessities.' (Acts 20:24.)

St Gregory does not raise the question of silence. Can the hermit sometimes receive visitors? Can he call on nearby hermits and talk with them about spiritual questions? St Christodoulos discourages such contacts; but in the world of the *Sayings of the Desert Fathers*, as on contemporary Athos, mutual visits between recluses are accepted as normal and even desirable. Needless to say, individual anchorites may feel the call, either temporarily or permanently, to complete silence. At one stage during his time in the forest St Seraphim spoke to no one; he did not open to visitors, and when anyone met him on the forest paths he lay on his face until they had gone away.

The programme outlined by St Gregory of Sinai is unquestionably severe, although not inhuman. Other hesychastic texts propose a more moderate regime. Kallistos and Ignatios Xanthopoulos (late fourteenth century) suggest that the hermit should spend the morning in reading and the afternoon in manual labour. Two meals are allowed, except on fast days; the hermit may sleep for five to six hours at night and may also take a short rest at midday.[39] These prescriptions about food and sleep correspond fairly closely to what would be demanded from a monk in a coenobium.

Many Eastern hermits have given especial attention to the reading of Holy Scripture. While in his forest retreat St Seraphim recited the full Divine Office and cultivated a small vegetable plot, while much of the night was spent reciting the Jesus Prayer. After his return to the monastery, when he was living enclosed in a cell, with no garden to look after, each week he read aloud the New Testament in its entirety: the Four Gospels on Monday to Thursday, Acts and the Epistles on Friday and Saturday.[40]

CONCLUSION

From this summary account of the hermit life in Orthodox Christendom, there emerge two points of particular relevance for the contemporary West:

(i) Whereas Western canon law regarding hermits has been marked until recently by an extreme rigidity, Eastern monasticism is distinguished in this as in other respects by flexibility and variety. In the practice of the Orthodox Church, no sharp line of demarcation is made between the solitary and the communal life. A hermit may be settled on the edge of an organized community—either a coenobium or a skete—returning to live in it for longer or shorter periods, and then going back into solitude. The degree of silence, enclosure and isolation varies greatly in the case of different solitaries, or at different periods in the same man's life. Such matters cannot and should not be made the subject of detailed legislation; freedom must be left to the conscience of the individual, guided by the Holy Spirit and by his spiritual father. Canon law should not displace the personal relationship between the abba and his disciple.

(ii) While hermits may depend directly on a coenobium, in the Christian East it is more usual for them to receive their pre-eremitic formation in a skete or kellion. The kelliot advances into seclusion by a series of gradual steps rather than by a single abrupt change; and at every step he is supported by continuing contacts with those living a more communal life in the skete. The role of the skete, in acting as a bridge between the solitary and the coenobitic life, is of cardinal importance. The present renewal of the hermit life in the West will surely go hand in hand with a revival of the skete system.

NOTES

1. *On Prayer* 124 (*PG* lxxix, 1193C). Evagrius gives this as a description of the monk, but he seems to have primarily in view the literal sense of the word *monachos*—one who lives alone (*monos*), the solitary.
    There is an English translation of this work by John Eudes Bamberger OCSO, *The Praktikos. Chapters on Prayer* (Cistercian Studies Series, No. 4: Spencer, Mass. 1972).

2. *The Ladder of Divine Ascent*, Step 1 (*PG* lxxxviii, 641D). See the English translation by Archimandrite Lazarus (Moore) (London 1959), p. 56.

3. Until recently eleven of the twenty monasteries were coenobitic and nine were idiorrhythmic. But in the last ten years three of these nine idiorrhythmic houses have returned to the coenobitic rule, and it is probable that more will do so in the coming decade.

4. They are to be found chiefly near the tip of the peninsula, on the wooded slopes above the Great Lavra and Kerasia. For a description of one such monk, see J. Valentin, *The Monks of Mount Athos* (London 1960), pp. 36-38.

5. Athanasius, *Life of Antony* (*PG* xxvi, 844B).

6. Ibid., 11 (860B).

7. *Apophthegmata*, Alphabetical Collection (hereafter 'Alph.'), Antony 37, 38 (*PG* lxv, 88B). Cf. English translation by Sr. Benedicta Ward SLG, *The Sayings of the Desert Fathers: The Alphabetical Collection* (Mowbrays 1975), p. 7.

8. Palladius, *Lausiac History* 22 (ed. C. Butler, pp. 70-73).

9. Pachomius, *Vita Prima* 6 (ed. F. Halkin, p. 4, lines 18-20).

10. Palladius, *Lausiac History* 7 & 38 (ed. Butler, p. 25, lines 10-14; p. 120, lines 7-8).

11. Alph., Longinus 1 (*PG* lxv, 256D); Sr. Benedicta, op. cit., p. 104.

12. *Apophthegmata*, Anonymous supplement, ed. F. Nau (hereafter 'Anon.'), no. 243 (*Revue de l'Orient chrétien*, xiv, 1909, p. 364); Sr. Benedicta Ward (trans.) *The Wisdom of the Desert Fathers* (Fairacres Publications, Oxford 1975), no. 111, p. 34.

13. Alph., Rufus 2 (*PG* lxv, 389C); cf. Sr Benedicta, *The Sayings of the Desert Fathers: Alph.*, p. 177.

14. Anon., 70 (*Revue de l'Orient chrétien* xii, 1907, p. 396).

15. *Praktikos* 5 (ed. A. and C. Guillaumont, *Sources chrétiennes* 171, pp. 504-5); trans. Bamberger, op. cit. (see n. 1), p. 16.

16. 'Fragments from the Life of Saint Seraphim', in G. P. Fedotov, *A Treasury of Russian Spirituality* (London 1950), p. 248.

17. *Ustav* (ed. Borovkova-Maikova), p. 88; cited in G. A. Maloney, *Russian Hesychasm: The Spirituality of Nil Sorskij*, (The Hague 1973), p. 111.

18. *Longer Rules* iii, 1 (*PG* xxxi, 917A). Cf. W. K. Lowther Clarke, *The Ascetic Works of Saint Basil* (London 1925), p.157.

19. *Longer Rules* vii, 4 (933B). Cf. Clarke, op. cit., p.166.

20. *Letter* 42 (*PG* xxxii, 348B-360B).

21. *Or.* xliii, 62 (*PG* xxxvi, 577B).

22. *Coll.* xviii, 16 (ed. E. Pichery, *Sources chrétiennes* 64, p. 36).

23. *Coll.* vii, 23 (ed. Pichery, *Sources chrétiennes* 42, pp.265-6).

24. *Inst.* viii, 18 (ed. J.-C. Guy, *Sources chrétiennes* 109, pp.358-9).

25. *Coll.* iii, 1; xviii, 15-16 (ed. Pichery, *Sources chrétiennes* 42, pp.139-40; ibid., 64, pp.28-36).

26. *Coll.* xix, 2 (ed. Pichery, *Sources chrétiennes* 64, pp.39-40).

27. *Rule* 73.

28. Cyril of Scythopolis, *Life of Euthymius* 31 (ed. E. Schwartz, *Texte und Untersuchungen* xlix, 2, p.50, lines 3-4). Similarly Euthymius does not allow the young Kyriakos to stay in the lavra, but sends him to the coenobium of Gerasimus: *Life of Kyriakos* 4 (ed. Schwartz, p.224, lines 23-25). There is a French translation of Cyril of Scythopolis by A.-J. Festugière OP, *Les Moines d'Orient*, vol. iii, 1-3 (Paris 1962-3).

29. Cyril, *Life of Sabas* 28-29 (ed. Schwartz, pp. 113-14).

30. Cyril, *Life of John the Hesychast* 6 (ed. Schwartz, p.206, lines 8-10).

31. This remarkable community is well described by D. J. Chitty, *The Desert a City* (Basil Blackwell, Oxford 1966), pp.132-40.

32. For Greek text and discussion of the canon, see Placide de Meester, *De Monachico Statu iuxta disciplinam byzantinam* (Sacra Congregazione per la Chiesa Orientale, Codificazione Canonica Orientale, Fonti Serie II — Fascicolo X: Rome 1942), pp.75-76, 312-13. (Council *in Trullo*: so called from *trullus*, meaning a dome, because it met in the domed hall of the imperial palace.)

33. For the *typikon* of the Great Lavra and related documents, see Ph. Meyer, *Die Haupturkunden für die Geschichte der Athosklöster* (Leipzig 1894), pp.102-40, esp. pp.115-16; for the *hypotyposis* of Patmos and connected material, see F. Miklosich and J.Müller, *Acta et diplomata graeca medii aevi*, vol. vi (Vienna 1890), pp.59-90. These documents are analysed by P. Dumont, 'Vie cénobitique ou vie hésychaste dans quelques "typica" byzantins', in *1054-1954. L'Église et les Églises. . . . Études et travaux . . . offerts à Dom Lambert Beauduin* (Chevetogne 1954), vol. ii, pp. 3-13.

34. These figures are taken from *Irénikon*, xliv, 4 (1971), p. 530. During the same year, the figures for Athos as a whole were as follows: out of a total of 1,145 monks, 446 were living in the twenty monasteries, 254 in the sketes, and 445 in isolated kalyvai and kellia. In these figures no distinction is made between the kelliots living together in small groups and the anchorites living alone; i.e.

between those following the semi-eremitic way and hermits in the strict sense. Indeed, such a distinction would be difficult to make in statistical tables, for the two classes shade into one another.

35. See Irina Gorainoff, 'Théoktistos', in *Contacts*, vol. xvii, no. 52 (1965), pp. 290-301; and 'Holy Men of Patmos', in *Sobornost*, series 6, no. 5 (1972), pp. 337-44.

36. *Chapters*, 99 and 101 (*PG* cl, 1272C-1273A); in the English translation of E. Kadloubovsky and G. E. H. Palmer, *Writings from the Philokalia on Prayer of the Heart* (London 1951), pp. 57-58.

37. See N. F. Robinson, *Monasticism in the Orthodox Churches* (London 1916), pp. 155-7.

38. *Chapters*, 102 (*PG* cl, 1273A); Kadloubovsky and Palmer, op. cit., p. 58.

39. *Century*, 25-27 (*PG* cxlvii, 684D-689A); Kadloubovsky and Palmer, op. cit., pp. 195-8.

40. Irina Gorainoff, *Séraphim de Sarov* (Collection 'Spiritualité Orientale', no. 11, Bellefontaine 1973), p. 53; also, by the same author, *The Message of Saint Seraphim* (Fairacres Publications, Oxford 1973), p. 6.

THE BIBLICAL BACKGROUND TO THE SOLITARY LIFE

ROLAND WALLS

RATHER THAN ATTEMPT the futile, and perhaps impossible task of looking for examples of Bible characters who had vocations to the life of solitude comparable to and paradigms of the great numbers of Christian solitaries, I will assume that what is wanted of this paper is a brief introduction to our reflection on the scriptural sources which traditionally have supported, and still sustain, this extreme and at first sight 'unchurchly' form of following Christ. We may assume that, during the long history of the eremitic life, extraneous motives and rationalizations from time to time infiltrated the tradition, sometimes with quite disastrous results. It is only too clear that some very unbiblical ideas were picked up on the way from Neoplatonism. So great was the subtlety of the fusion of these with the genuine tradition, that it was often only the simple faith of the lay hermit, who remained apart from the sophistications of those who left their mark on the literary search for a rationale of the life, that saved the day.

Only a rough conspectus of the main areas of the Bible, which have provided solitaries from the time of the Desert Fathers to the present day with ample room for reflection on the proper setting of their life in the content and form of the revelation, can be attempted here. The review will be systematic rather than historical.

REVELATION

It was often to the solitary servant of God that the Lord revealed himself and his plans. Abraham was alone when he received the three messengers and found he had encountered his God. He is brought out under the night stars to be given the promise of a destiny in his offspring. Moses in the solitude of the desert, with sheep as his only companions, stands barefooted before the theophany of Israel's God in the burning bush, and later in the same desert is called up the mountain alone to meet again the God who affirms in the giving of the Law the covenant with his people. Elijah the patron of hermits detaches himself from the schools of the prophets to take his lonely journey into the desert to experience the providence of God, and later he goes alone in the strength of the meal

48

provided by the angel to Horeb where in the solitude of the cave he hears the Voice of God in the voice of silence. Not only in these classic passages but throughout the Old Testament there is a link between solitude and revelation. The servant of God has to enter the solitude of God to receive the news that God has determined to form and to be with his community. In order to fulfil his role within the society of Israel the prophet has to enter the experience of loneliness—often physical and always spiritual—so that men may enjoy community. This of course adumbrates the climax of the loneliness of the God-Man at the crucifixion, the birthplace of the new communal humanity.

This theme of the paradox of the solitary recipient of revelation apart from and on behalf of the community recurs in the New Testament. There is perhaps no mystery so congenial to the contemplative solitary as that of the Transfiguration of Christ. Here there are so many facets that it would be impossible to do justice to them all in a short review. The tradition has loved to dwell on the threefold emphasis of the apostles being called *apart, by themselves alone*; on their seeing no man but Jesus only; on the experience being of the glory of the Last Day and on the silent entry into the cloud of the Divine Presence. But the health of the conscious privilege of being called up the mountain of the Transfiguration has been scripturally assured when the tradition has also dwelt on the identity of the three with Christ on Tabor with the three that were with him in Gethsemane—on both occasions finding themselves absurdly inadequate.

Another mystery of Christ, rightly treasured by solitaries to the present day, is the Presentation of Christ in the Temple, which was the occasion of the fruition of the lonely, waiting, temple-dwelling lives of Simeon and Anna who in their poverty of spirit were ready to receive and to acknowledge Christ on behalf of expectant Israel.

A principal scriptural patron of the solitaries is St John the beloved disciple who lay on the bosom of Christ—who himself lies in the bosom of the Father—and whose enforced but divinely planned solitude on Patmos was the occasion of the revelation of the End of this age and of the Lord's eighth day after the completed series of sevens, which through woes and birthpangs brought the people of God into the final community with him in the City and in the Garden. With John, the two Maries—who significantly stood with him by the Cross of Jesus—give inspiration and character to the eremitic vocation. Mary Magdalene, identified universally in the tradition with Mary the sister of Martha, received the seal of Christ's blessing on her contemplative leisure, and her lonely, passionate seeking was rewarded by the first appearance of the Risen Christ. Above all, it was the Mother of Jesus who gave the pattern of the true exercise of the solitary when she kept all these things and pondered them in her heart.

Solitude, and the leaving of all for God, even the community on behalf of which this withdrawal is made, is closely bound up—as we have already noted—with the giving of revelation in Scripture, and it is the function of the solitary to renew in himself, as the Holy, revealing, Spirit determines, the moment of the revelation given once for all, and yet again and again offered to us for acceptance and understanding. The solitary is a reminder to the Church that tradition alone, or the teaching offices, cannot of themselves guarantee to each age the pristine freshness of what God not only has shown, but still shows. This revelatory aspect of the hermit's vocation removes him from that ever-present danger of reducing his role to the requirements of personal devotion, either of his own or of others. He is where he is for a radical purpose, related to the contemporary reception of the revelation by the faith of the present-day Church.

His existence is a reminder of the spiritually and often physically lonely patriarch or prophet whose solitude is itself a witness to the single-minded purity of heart which is needed to see God, whose transcendence no created thing can image. Communal theophany is unusual in the Bible, but all theophany is for community. The solitude of the hermit is therefore never private.

PREPARATION FOR THE KINGDOM

If the eremitic tradition had a source of strength and illumination in these high moments of theophany and revelation, it was especially so with regard to the role and character of John the Baptist, the patron *par excellence* of the solitary. Just as John lived as a stranger to the ways of men to prepare for a kingdom which was not a continuation or mere fulfilment of any kingdom of man but a radically discontinuous order and rule, so the solitary witnesses to the essential otherness of the Kingdom of God. The Church, whose function is to proclaim the Kingdom, is preserved from the folly of compromise with the world in so far as she heeds and cherishes the strange scandal of the solitary vocation. Moreover, John's preparation, both in his own person and in his preaching, was not one calling for human achievement but rather a life-long acknowledgement of man's need for self-emptying and effacement before God in penitence and hard living.

John and the solitaries who succeed him have no function in man's city; their only reference and relevance are to the reign of God. They ensure that we do not mis-read the message of the incarnation by thinking that God joins us on our own terms and without remainder. They are called to live out *in extremis* the words of Christ: 'My Kingdom is not of this world.'

COMBAT

Because of their relation to the revealing activity of God and to the preparation for the future kingdom, solitaries have traditionally seen their calling in terms of the conflict with the enemy of God and man. The desert is not only the place where Israel's God is encountered but it is there that the forces of darkness muster. If Jacob wrestles in prayer with God alone in the desert of Peniel, it is in the desert of Judaea that Christ meets his adversary. In the wilderness of solitude the hermit is not surprised to find the devil. He has deliberately, at the call of God, gone out with the full armour of God, to do battle with him as he attempts to succeed with the servants of God where he failed with the Son of God.

The realism which soon banishes any romantic notions we may have at the beginning of the solitary life comes from an understanding of this biblical theme, unknown to the Neoplatonist, or to the self-regarding choices of those disillusioned with the human race. The solitary is placed in the situation where the temptations of self-pleasing and self-preoccupation are at their most acute, and it is there that he has to struggle with the demonic assaults on the spirit as well as on the flesh. Therefore the combat merges into the final *agonia* and experience of dereliction as the privilege of the mountain is succeeded by the demands of Gethsemane to keep awake and pray with Christ, to endure that fierce stripping of the will until it has nothing left but the Will of God. Only by such scriptural understanding of his calling is he prepared for that dark blessing when he is allowed to share something of the dereliction of Christ and to find his festival in Holy Saturday. Buried with Christ in the solitude and silence of his cell—which the Desert Fathers called a tomb—he demonstrates in an extreme form the truth behind the existence of the Church. Any life that emerges from this buried life can only be Resurrection life, a sheer gift of God which faith alone can receive.

The eremitic life is in essence a grain of salt, a silent reminder to the Church of the exigencies of her life in Christ if she is not to incur the judgement of having become tasteless. The costly interiority of the follow-

D

ing of Christ on his way to the Father must accompany the proclamation of what Christ has done for us once for all. The solitary gains stability in his vocation in so far as he understands the Christological and baptismal import of what he is undertaking, and that it is not for himself alone but with and for the whole Body.

For this he puts himself under those conditions where total trust in God is demanded, in that desert which is the primal scriptural symbol of the absence of all human aid and comfort; where God alone can open the fountain for Hagar or send the ravens to Elijah; where God alone can sustain the journey of his chosen people to the promised land.

UNION WITH GOD

If there is one complete book of the Bible which, apart from the Psalter, was and still is a mainstay of the solitary, it is the Song of Songs. The curious inclusion of this love poem in Holy Scripture has resulted in a rich history of interpretation which has nourished the roots of the eremitic life from the beginning. This is because solitude has no final meaning if it is not the solitude of the lover either in search of or in the company of the beloved. Here the story of the single-minded quest and the joyful finding affords just the parable of the solitary life. Without this final explanation of the love for the Beloved the meaning of the other facets would be incomplete. Faith and hope cannot stand without charity. Once again mere personal devotion is not the whole story, for the classical interpretation is not primarily concerned with the soul's love for God but with God's love for man, the love of Christ for his Church and therefore her love for him. The scriptural solitary understands his life both as his personal love lived in solitude, and as a lived icon of the substance of the final mystery of the eternal intentions of God. 'Love is all His meaning.'

It is here we can begin to see why the Christian solitary must find his meaning in community and not in any flight of the alone to the Alone, why he must be open to charity both to God and man—to hospitality if need be, to necessary good works, and to openness towards the Church through his spiritual father and his bishop. It is his supreme task to live out the deep mysteries of God's love in Christ.

It would be out of the question to conclude this brief review of the biblical background to the solitary life without dwelling for a moment on the Psalms, the solitary's prayer book. The staple offering of praise, thanksgiving, penitence, and petition takes the same form as that of the universal Church, of Israel, of Christ himself. Alone, but never alone, the hermit joins all suffering, sinful, despairing, as well as happy, humanity in articulating its unsaid prayer. He is, through his solitude, united to the praying Church through the praying Christ. It is the Psalter more than anything else that has preserved the essentially corporate and communal aspect of the Christian solitary and prevented him from escaping into a life abysmally concerned with soul culture, or losing his identity among undifferentiated contemplatives of all religions.

And no doubt that same Psalter which expresses his unbreakable link with the Church and with all men will also express, in words he will find hard to better, the inexpressible joy of his own particular calling.

> *One thing have I desired of the Lord which I will require, even that I may dwell in the house of the Lord all the days of my life, that I may behold the fair beauty of the Lord and to visit his temple. For in the time of trouble he shall hide me in his tabernacle, yea in the secret place of his dwelling he shall hide me and set me up upon a rock of stone.*
>
> *Ps. 27*

THE RELATIONSHIP BETWEEN HERMITS AND COMMUNITIES
IN THE WEST
WITH SPECIAL REFERENCE TO THE TWELFTH CENTURY

SISTER BENEDICTA WARD SLG

IN THE SECOND HALF of the eleventh century, Peter Damian, the Prior of
Fonte Avellana, wrote about a problem recently raised in his community:
'Many of the brethren, followers of the eremitic life, have asked me
whether, since they live alone in their cells, it is right for them to say
Dominus vobiscum, Jube, domne, benedicere, and the like, despite the fact
that they are alone.' He goes on to answer the question himself with a long
letter on the hermit life which is known as 'The Book of the Lord Be With
You'[1] in which he included the following passage as the kernel of his
argument:

> He [the hermit] sees as present with the eyes of the spirit all those
> for whom he prays . . . he knows that all who are praying with him
> are present in spritual communion . . . Therefore let no brother who
> lives alone in a cell be afraid to utter words which are common to
> the whole Church, for although he is separated by space from the
> congregation of the faithful, yet he is bound together with them all
> by love in the unity of the faith; although they are absent in the
> flesh, they are near at hand in the mystical unity of the Church.[2]

In examining the exact ways in which hermits were connected with communities in external matters, it is essential to have in mind that these
external links are meant to subserve and express that deep inner unity in
which the hermit is 'bound together with them all by love in the unity of
the faith'. When a monk goes to live apart from his brothers it is possible
to note and mark the ways in which he is separate from them, but what
cannot be assessed in terms of legislation is the main part of his life which
is concerned with affirming his unity in Christ with them all; in the mysterious words of St Antony, the father of hermits, 'my life is with my
neighbour'.

On the level of external contact between hermits and society, however,
this fundamental spiritual link has been expressed in different ways in
different ages. I would like to examine here the tradition within monasticism

in the West in the Middle Ages, with special reference to some developments in the twelfth century. The material is taken mostly from the lives of saints but I have also tried to show how the relationship between hermits and society was viewed in theory as well as in practice.

The Rule of Saint Benedict was the basis of Christian monasticism from the eighth century to the eleventh. It is often supposed that this Rule formally excluded the idea of the hermit life, and a superficial reading of the text in itself supports this claim. However, no Rule can be assessed truly simply by its written words, and there is ample evidence that hermits continued to exist within the Benedictine tradition and to find their justification within the Rule itself. Cassiodorus, like Jerome and Cassian, had seen the hermit life as a stage within the monastic life, and at Vivarium he provided hermitages for this purpose;[3] it appeared to the early Benedictines that this was the teaching also of the Rule of Saint Benedict. In the first chapter of the Rule, four kinds of monks are discussed, and though the Rule provides most of all for the 'strong race of cenobites'[4] the hermits are described as the end-product of the cenobitic life:

> After long probation in the monastery, having learnt in association with many brethren how to fight against the devil, [they] go out well-armed from the ranks of the community to the solitary combat of the desert. They are now able to live without the help of others, and by their own strength and God's assistance to fight against the temptations of mind and body.[5]

The monastery is 'a school of the Lord's service'[6] in which men attain 'some degree of virtue and the rudiments of monastic observance'[7]; but the Rule claims only to be 'a little Rule for beginners'.[8] For those who 'hasten to the perfection of the monastic life', St Benedict recommends 'the teaching of the holy Fathers . . . the Conferences of Cassian, and his Institutes, and the Lives of the Fathers and also the Rule of our holy father, Basil'.[9] St Benedict himself lived as a hermit, and it is probable that at Monte Cassino there were, as at Vivarium, separate cells for hermits. In the following centuries it is clear that there were hermits attached to monastic houses as a matter of course and, though the perils of such a life and its rarity were increasingly recognized, there is constant evidence of its existence. Grimlaicus, in his Rule for solitaries in the ninth century says, 'to enter the solitary life is the highest perfection; to live imperfectly in solitude is to incur the greatest damnation'.[10] Archeological discoveries have given evidence of hermitages around monasteries, and particularly near Cluny, which was as much a centre for hermit life as for liturgical devotion.[11] Many chroniclers describe hermits, and the fact of their existence is apparent from many saints' lives. Conciliar decrees and monastic customaries tried to exercise some control over the entry of monks into such a life and over their subsequent activities. These hermits had been monks and, after living in a monastery for some time they went, with the blessing of their abbot, to live alone or with one or two companions. Their lives are described in terms familiar from the fourth century and the beginnings of monasticism; solitude, prayer, ascetic practices, and simplicity of life were their characteristics. In the reasons for their choice of such a life and in the paths that led them there they differed widely. There was, for instance, Wulsi of Evesham, a layman who was professed at Crowland in the eleventh century, and who found himself unable to participate in the liturgical and administrative life of a large community; he became a hermit in a cave near Evesham. On the other hand, Maurus, a former abbot of Fulda, chose to enter the eremitical life because he would have leisure there for study.[12] There were monks trained in the East who settled as hermits in the midst of the Western cenobitic communities, like Symeon of Trier and Constantine of Malmesbury, and both were accepted and praised. There were hermits who received the blessing of their abbot to embrace a life of solitude permanently; there were also part-time hermits. Notably, there were bishops and abbots, busy administrators, who had cells to which they could retire. Hermedland, first Abbot of Aindre, always spent Lent in solitude and at the end of his life retired permanently to a hermitage.[13]

There was a peaceful relationship of concord between these hermits and their communities. At times a hermit might be recalled because of the needs of his house, most of all if he were needed as abbot for a time. Monks would visit their hermits and consult them on spiritual matters, and some of the hermits found it proper to their vocation to return to the monastery for the liturgy on Sundays and feast days. Hermits were relatively few, and it was because the numbers remained small that this peaceful co-existence was possible. Customaries sometimes legislated for a percentage of hermits only, out of a community at any time, and this was never more than ten per cent. In all this the tradition both of the West and of the East does not seem to diverge: the hermit was a monk who sought solitude for a longer or shorter time, who maintained links with the monastery in certain ways, and who was allowed for the rest to follow out his vocation as an individual however God called him. It is with the twelfth century that there is a change, and this is closely connected with what is often called the 'crisis of coenobitism' in the West.

It is clear that in the twelfth century a new type of hermit emerged. The traditional pattern of a monk who entered on the hermit life after training in the monastery was still recognized on the same terms as before, but there were many also who had either never been monks or who had found the monastic life in some way unacceptable. With these new hermits a distinction was made between monks and hermits along sharper and less amicable lines. The problems involved were complex and to some extent meant that the term hermit and also the term monk were being re-defined. Since the influence of this is still with us, especially in our concepts of contemplative communities, a closer look at this movement is essential.

There were, first, those who began the hermit life without monastic training. Then there were those who had been monks but had undertaken a hermit way of life more or less as a clearing ground until a concept of community again emerged for them. In the first group there were three famous English hermits: Wulfric of Haselbury, Christina of Markyate, and Godric of Finchale. All of them began their hermit lives outside the monastic structures, though all of them developed close relationships with communities later. Wulfric[14] was born of a middle-class English family in the reign of William Rufus at Compton Martin in Somerset. He was ordained below the canonical age and lived as a careless and worldly cleric at Deverill near Warminster where he neglected his duties for hunting. In about 1125 he underwent a conversion, and was also offered the cure of the village where he had been born. There, under the protection of William Fitzwalter, he became an anchorite in a cell in the wall of the church where he lived until his death. The villagers supported him, and turned to him for spiritual advice, and possibly for practical help since it seems at least possible to deduce from his life that his cell was used as a kind of strong room in which villagers could safely leave their money in the troubled times of King Stephen. Wulfric was known to St Bernard by repute and was approved by him. He was consulted by kings and lords as well as local people, and he had some connection with both the local Cluniac priory of Montacute and the Cistercian house at Ford. The monks of Montecute tried to claim his body after his death, but he was in fact buried in his cell. John, a monk of Ford, wrote his life with admiration and affection.

Like Wulfric, Christina of Markyate[15] did not enter a novitiate in a religious house. This may well have been because she had literally no chance to do so. The opposition of her parents, lack of a dowry, and the prohibition of her doing so by the bishop, debarred her from any monastic house whatever. In order to fulfil her desire for a life of consecrated virginity, she ran away from home and lived among a close net-work of hermits who inhabited the district around St Albans. She joined at first a woman recluse, Alfwen, a hermitess at Flamstead; after two years she went to live with the hermit Roger at Markyate. Roger was one of a remarkable group of hermits who lived near the Abbey of St Albans, and from them Christina received her training as a hermit. After Roger's death she continued, after a year elsewhere, at Markyate and soon made contact with Geoffrey, the Abbot of St Albans. Roger had been a monk of St Albans, and Christina's connections with the monastery were close; it seems almost certain that the St Albans' psalter was written at St Albans for her use. Her friendship with Abbot Geoffrey was deep and continuous, and she was regarded by the other monks as a spiritual guide. It is, however, notable that she did not make her profession as a nun until 1131, after living for many years as a hermit and after being offered the abbatial office at St Clements, York. Her profession, moreover, was made in the monastery at St Albans. Women joined her at Markyate, and though the account of her life breaks off before the death of Geoffrey, it is clear that she continued as a recognized and able abbess for the rest of her life.

Godric of Finchale[16] was an English merchant and sailor who was converted to a more serious Christianity in Jerusalem. He visited Rome, Compostella and Jerusalem, and finally returned to his native Northumbria, where he simply went and lived in solitude. Some land at Finchale was leased to him by the Bishop of Durham, and he also made contact on a spiritual level with the Durham monks. After some years he decided to place himself under obedience to the Prior of Durham, and a more definite relationship with the community emerged. The Prior sent a monk to say mass at the hermitage every feast day, and Reginald, Godric's biographer, a monk of Durham, visited him at those times and also was with him when he became ill at the end of his life. A priory of Durham was established eventually at Finchale.

These hermits were part of a new eremitic pattern, and a more famous one of the same kind shows how this solitude could emerge into a new form of community. Stephen of Muret[17] learned about monastic life while visiting the monks of Calabria, but he did not become a monk in any formal sense. Instead, he went alone to a mountain near Muret and there professed himself. His biographer says:

> He had a ring with which he espoused himself to Christ, saying: 'I, Stephen, renounce the devil and all his pomps, and devote myself to God, Father, Son and Holy Spirit, God Three and One, Living and True'. He also wrote out this formula and placed it on his head saying: 'I, Stephen, promise to serve God in this desert in the Catholic faith, and for this cause I place this form upon my head and this ring on my finger that at the day of my death it may be unto me according to my promise. . . . I ask you, Lord, to restore to me the wedding garment and count me among the sons of the Church at the wedding feast of your Son.'[18]

Other solitaries joined Stephen and the Order of Grandmont was formed. The Grandmontines kept the eremitic life as their basic aim; all the administration was in the hands of the *conversi*, and a standard of evangelical poverty was maintained which foreshadowed that of the Franciscans later. They claimed to follow only the Gospel and not even the Fathers. Their solitude, however, was like that which evolved for other hermits, a corporate solitude, in which each member of the group lived in varying degrees of personal solitude; but the characteristic feature of them as a group was that they were apart from society.

These four did not pass through any formal novitiate nor was their link with the older monastic communities that of formal training and profession. The hermit life was not for them the final stage of a monastic vocation in which they were living out their monastic life under different conditions but basically still as an integral part of their community. They are typical of the new understanding of hermit life in the twelfth century. Stephen of Grandmont provides a link between this kind of new hermit and the more famous kind who were hermit-founders. The new monastic Orders of Camaldoli, Chartreuse, Savigny, Fontrevault, and above all, Cîteaux, were the end product of the hermit explosion of the early years of the twelfth century. Besides these, over fifty other communities which adopted a communal rule of life began from hermit foundations. For instance, there was a group of hermits at Llanthony early in the twelfth century, and by 1120 they had become a house of canons following the Rule of

St Augustine with customs from Aldgate, Colchester and Merton.[19] Besides these, many houses of hermits became affiliated to Cîteaux, including Morimond and Pontigny.

The founders of these communities lived at first as hermits. Romuald, the founder, with Ludolph and Julian, of Fonte Avellana, tried first of all to persuade his community at St Appolinaris in Classe to adopt his ideas, then left it to live alone until a new community formed around him.[20] John Gualbert lived as a hermit at Vallombrosa, and the monastery that grew there continued to be known as the Hermitage, both because of its austerity and its remoteness from the world. Stephen of Obazine, Bruno of Cologne, and Vitalis of Savigny all contemplated a form of solitude which was not that of existing communities. Two things distinguished their idea of hermit life from that of the more traditional hermits: first, their concept of corporate solitude; and secondly, their desire for stability and obedience to recognized authority among themselves. The idea of solitude in a group is different from the idea of personal solitude. St Norbert said, like any hermit in any age, 'I do not want to stay in the towns; I prefer places that are deserted and uncultivated'.[21] But he did not expect to stay in the desert alone. Vitalis of Savigny withdrew to the 'desert', but it was in company with other recluses.[22] The desire for obedience was a corporate ideal, and when combined with the new concept of solitude as being simply away from the towns, led to the evolution of hermits into communities.

Of the new communities, Camaldoli, Chartreuse, Fonte Avellana, and Grandmont came closest to the Eastern concept of a lavra, though with more monks than was usual in the East. The brothers lived in separate cells and the degree of communal life was minimal. At Fonte Avellana, for instance, they met only on Sundays for Mass and Office, while at the Grande Chartreuse they only sang the Office of Vigils together. At Grandmont the separation of the group as a whole from the rest of the world included a stress upon absolute individual solitude as well. The monks in these groups were called hermits. It was not envisaged that they would move on to a greater personal solitude; it was a corporate life in which it was held that the hermit ideal was already realised. It is possible to see this kind of group as a restoration, almost certainly an unconscious restoration, of the idea of the skete which had fallen out of use in the West, the difference being that whereas the Eastern skete was a stage towards the complete hermit life, the hermits of Camaldoli and Chartreuse were basically committed to their monastery. The most famous of these new communities was, of course, Cîteaux, and the differences between the old and new forms of monastic life received dramatic publicity as a conflict between the Cluniacs and Cistercians. The Cistercians were, more than any of the new Orders, concerned to integrate solitude into community. They began as a group of hermits, and called their new home a 'desert'; hermits individually and in groups were to join them later. But the Cistercian way of life was basically inimical to the concept of individual solitude. The Order of Cîteaux claimed to have found the 'more perfect way' of St Benedict's Rule and to have embodied it in their corporate life. This idea of integrated solitude could cause difficulty when members joined who discovered a desire in themselves for the traditional hermit withdrawal; it was seen as a reproach, as opting out of what all wanted and had, and in this it is possible to see the problems that later faced contemplative communities whose members sought greater solitude from a context which *de facto* claimed to have it already.

The hermits formed communities, and with this they posed a new question about the meaning of the term 'hermit'. The topic gave ample scope to the twelfth century's attrait for categorization, but in discussions of the matter the hermit escaped too rigid definition in a significant way. The *Libellus de Ordinibus Diversis*, for instance, lays the stress in differentiating between monk and hermit on the life itself: 'I do not argue much about the name when I see the works performed . . . without the life the name alone is empty'.[23] The term hermit is in this treatise extended to include the new hermit communities. The monk, the writer says, is a hermit when he goes into the desert with like-minded men: 'He will penetrate the innermost part of the desert with Antony where he will merit the aid of the angels against the demons and the company of good men following him for God's sake; when you have done well you must go out into the mountain with Jesus and pass the night there in prayer.' It seems that by the end of the twelfth century the hermit was beginning to be defined as 'ascetic' rather than as one who lives alone. The most extreme example I know of this re-definition is in the accounts of the martyrdom of Archbishop Thomas Becket at Canterbury. When the monks stripped the dead body of this man who had not in life been notable for solitude, either corporate or personal, they discovered that he had worn a hair shirt. 'Lo,' they exclaimed, 'here indeed was a true monk *and hermit.*'[24]

The evidence of the hermit movements in the West in the twelfth century points to several conclusions. First, there is the overall tendency to understand the hermit life as no longer exclusively the summit of monastic life in community. Two aspects of this appear and lead in different directions, both of which have their bearing on contemporary approaches to eremitism in the Church. There were, first of all, those who saw the hermit life as a preliminary to life in community, and from these there emerges a new understanding of the relationship between community and solitary in which the stress is placed upon the solitude of the group rather than the individual. It is from these groups who tried to embody the ideals of solitude within communities that the modern 'contemplative' communities derive in at least certain aspects; and the problems posed for these communities with regard to the individual hermit remain. Secondly, however, hermits were known in the twelfth century who had never undergone any religious training in a community and whose relationship with the monks was not necessarily of a formal nature. This underlines the essentially free and unstructured nature of the hermit vocation and serves to emphasise the fact that there will always be in the Church those whom God calls into the wilderness and keeps there for their love of the Crucified to overflow in ways of prayer. That is the service Peter Damian speaks of in the quotation with which this paper began. It is then for the monks and for the Church to enable them to remain hidden within the quiver of his love.

NOTES

1. Peter Damian, 'The Book of the Lord Be With You', trans. Patricia McNulty in *Peter Damian, Selected Writings*, Faber 1959, pp. 53-4.

2. Ibid., pp. 73-4.

3. Cassiodorus, *Institutiones*, ed. R.A.B. Mynors, Oxford 1937, p. 74.

4. *The Rule of St Benedict*, ed. and trans. J. McCann, London 1952, p. 16.

5. Ibid., cap. 1, p. 14.

6. Ibid., Prologue, p. 12.

7. Ibid., cap. 73, p. 160.

8. Ibid., cap. 73, p. 162.

9. Ibid., cap. 73, p. 160.

10. Grimlaicus, *Regula Solitarium*, cap. 23, *PL* CIII, col. 604.

11. I am greatly indebted for information about Cluny and about the hermit movements as a whole to an unpublished thesis by Henrietta Leyser, 'The New Eremitical Movements in Western Europe, 1000–1150' (Oxford, 1966).

12. Rudolph, *Miracula sanctorum in Fuldenses ecclesias translatorum, Monumenta Germaniae Historica, Scriptores*, XV, i, p. 340.

13. *Vita S. Hermelandi abb. Antrens, Acta Sanctorum Ordinis S. Benedicti*, ed. Mabillon, III, i, p. 396.

14. John of Ford, *Life of Wulfric of Haslebury*, ed. Dom Maurice Bell, Somerset Record Society, vol. XLVII, 1933.

15. *Christina of Markyate*, ed. and trans. C. Talbot, Oxford 1959.

16. Reginald of Durham, *Libellus de vita et miraculis S. Godrici*, ed. J. Stevenson, Surtees Society XX (1845).

17. *Vita S. Stephani confessoris (Muretensis) PL* CCIV, cols. 1013 ff.

18. Ibid., col. 1016.

19. J. Dickinson, *The Origins of the Austin Canons*, SPCK 1950, pp. 111-12.

20. Peter Damian, *Vita Romualdi, PL* CXLV, col. 336.

21. Herman, *Liber III de miraculis S. Mariae Laudenensis*, cap. 3, *Monumenta Germaniae Historica, Scriptores*, XII, p. 656.

22. Ordericus Vitalis, *Historia Ecclesiastica*, Bk. VIII, cap. 27, ed. A. le Prévost and L. Delisle, Paris, (1838-1855), p. 449.

23. *Libellus de Ordinibus Diversis*, ed. Constable and Smith, Oxford 1972, p. 26.

24. *Materials for the History of Archbishop Thomas Becket*, ed. J. C. Robertson (Rolls Series, 1875-1833) vol. I, 12.

EREMITICAL REVIVAL IN THE ANGLICAN CHURCH
IN THE TWENTIETH CENTURY

MOTHER MARY CLARE SLG

INTRODUCTION

This paper is essentially a personal testimony of experience gained through my own community as part of the recovery of the eremitical life in the Anglican Church as a whole. In this century we find the dedication of men and women to this way of life coinciding with the catastrophic years which began with the First World War, for the solitary is called to be at that point of conflict where good and evil meet. Parallel to this was the rise of contemplative communities in the Anglican Church called to the same conflict.

We are gathered here in St David's to pray together and to rejoice together in the eremitical tradition. We are truly brothers and sisters in Christ from whatever part of his Body we come. We rejoice in our unity and give thanks to God in the Holy Spirit who is the source of our prayer and fraternal charity, and we meet in the fellowship of all God's saints who have in every age borne witness

> to his sovereignty;
> to the fundamental Gospel precepts;
> to the penitent life expressed by silence and hiddenness;
> to the spirit of spontaneity
> with the application of common sense and discretion;
> in a life of perfect charity.

It is especially fitting that we should be gathered in St David's where one of the Anglican women solitaries of the 1930s came from Festiniog to live her suffering life of prayer for all mankind. I quote from a personal letter of hers which will remind us that we are praying and conferring on the very ground where for centuries the eremitical tradition has not been lost.

> One feels indeed that one treads on holy ground and lives on it. It is wonderful too to realise that here the solitary life is not only justified but accepted to this day. St David and his companions lived as solitaries in little stone huts round the first primitive cathedral—

64

burnt down, alas!—but the sort of thing is still to be seen in the remains of St Non's Chapel. St Non, the mother of St David, lived as a solitary on the cliff overlooking St Non's Bay, which is part of St Bride's Bay, most lovely. Close by is St Non's Well, still intact, the whole place being the oldest religious building in Wales. It is only about twenty minutes walk from the Cathedral, so she would have been able to go to Mass. Then St Justinian, St David's greatest friend, who was a priest at the Cathedral, became a hermit and his chapel is on the cliffs about two miles away. Further on is St Patrick's Chapel. Then in the Cathedral itself, there are many tombs but only two shrines—places of pilgrimage. One, of course, is St David's; the other that of St Caradoc, hermit, who lived more than 500 years after him. St David died in 601, St Caradoc in 1124.

Sister Mary Fidelia, Solitary of the Holy Spirit, was not alone in her witness to the solitary life. Sister Adeline Cashmore was another Anglican recluse of the same period living her saintly life of hidden prayer and intercession at East Harptree. She was described by one who knew her, and was himself her confessor, as 'one of the merriest people I ever knew', and by Father William of Glasshampton, himself a solitary, as 'a pure spirit, on fire with love for God'.

Sister Mary Fidelia had a successor as a solitary in North Wales who set up her anchorhold in the village of Dolgellau and who finally died in Oxford under the care of the Wantage Sisters in 1958. There is to this day an anchoress in a wooden hut in the grounds of the Shrine of Our Lady at Walsingham; and of the thousands who flock to that place of pilgrimage the majority are unaware of her presence and unceasing intercession. I am making no mention of those members of other Anglican communities where individual members are living under special conditions of solitude and silence.

At the present time there is a renewal of interest in the eremitical way of life, partly because of the strain of modern society and partly because of the reassessment of the religious life after Vatican II. Since then many have desired to return to the ascesis of silence, to the positive, creative use of silence, and to explore the deeper levels of prayer. Some of these, laity and religious, want to enter contemplative communities, others to have 'houses of prayer' within communities; but some have an actual desire to rediscover the secret of the desert—a secret only found in the depths of *metanoia* and purity of heart. This involves conflict.

I

What I want to say in this section is comprised in a passage from Jean Daniélou's book, *The Lord of History:*

> The Constantinian phase of Christian history is coming to an end: the old Christian world, or worldly Christianity, is breaking up under the irresistible pressure of new and vital forces. The Christians who see this most clearly are those who bear the heat and burden of the workers' day: they feel a much closer affinity with the early Church than with medieval Christendom or with the Age of Reason. . . . And this also furnishes the complete explanation of something else, a development which I take to be peculiarly characteristic of our own time, namely the re-entry of contemplatives into the active life of the world. For in the early days of Christianity, the holy virgins and the men of prayer lived their daily lives as part of the one Christian community in full contact with the world of paganism. The flight into the desert was a revolutionary innovation, dating from the fourth century, when St Antony inaugurated the age of monks, the withdrawal of the contemplatives from a world in which Christianity was compromised, into the solitudes where they might keep alive the faith of the martyrs. That age is passing— St Antony is coming back from his desert; there is no need for flight now that the Church is once again an army of martyrs, in the midst of a heathen society. 'My factory is my desert.'
>
> (op. cit. Longmans, Green and Co. 1958, p.77)

In this soulless age the desert can be found in the utter aloneness of the city, in a single room in a high-rise block of flats in an industrial area. People will come to those living under such conditions if they are making a valid witness and can truly be seen to be seeking God. Daniélou goes on: 'For a Christian who has to live among men whose preoccupations, under Marxist influences, are exclusively materialistic, the main difficulty will be to preserve his faith in moral and spiritual values.' That surely is the reason why our religious communities, whether active or contemplative, should be very sure of their priorities, and that they 'stand before all men on behalf of the Church, bearing witness to the presence of God within and beyond all things, and to the coming of the Kingdom'.*

*From a Working Party Paper commissioned by the Anglican Advisory Council, SPCK 1970.

Granted the initial impetus to live the solitary life may be deliberately chosen and permission sought as part of a personal quest yet, if the vocation is a genuine one, this personal search—not only the search for God, though it is always that—must develop into a quest that brings us to a place where we are exposed to a deep heart-searching, a listening awareness of the fundamental crying need of the world. This is the monk or nun's chief service to mankind at all times and is to be most experienced by the solitary.

In aloneness we learn to share in a basic way in the emptiness and lost-ness that modern man often knows, but also tries to block out and ignore. The solitary, though he may spend much time alone is *never* alone in the sense of being alienated from humanity, unaware of its sorrows and agonies and unmindful of his responsibility to bring persons, known and unknown, to the mercy of God through prayer. As 'watchmen upon the walls' the solitaries are at the point where the forces of evil and the redemptive power of God meet. This means that the solitary must be a still centre who does not react to others' reactions.

The eremitical vocation, therefore, as those not personally called by God to such a way sometimes imagine, cannot be the desire to seek one's own salvation nor to contract out of the spread of the Gospel of the Body of Christ. On the contrary, the vocation lies at the very centre of the heart of the Church for, as the Vatican II 'Constitution on Liturgy' decrees: 'It belongs to the Church to be both human and divine, visible but rich in invisible realities, fervent in action yet fully contemplative, present in this world and yet a stranger to it; but in such a way that that which is to her in any way human is ordered, is submitted to what is divine.'

The function of the charisma of the solitary life is to express openly this interior aspect of the mystery of the Church which is its intimate and personal relationship with Christ, a sharing in his passion and his glory. In the heart of the Church, therefore, the life of the hermit is exposed to the Spirit by whose power the fulness of his gifts are made fruitful for all mankind. In the measure that he allows the Spirit free action in himself the ascetic is enabled to intercede for his brothers to whom he already manifests on earth the presence of the kingdom of God.

For the solitary, the words of St Antony, the father of hermits, become a living reality: 'My life is with my neighbour.' So the solitary is in the forefront of the fray, with no other arms than prayer and penitence.

Although alone, he is one with all his brothers who in their way labour to hasten the coming of the kingdom. He is, according to Evagrius, separated from all and united to all.

In some of the Anglican communities today there are those who are seeking ways and means to express both the corporate and the individual desire for greater solitude and silence, more prayer and a deeper participation in Christ's ministry of reconciliation. We can find at least one reason why this should be so in an extract from the religious article by Angela Tilby in *The Times* of 24 August 1974:

> If the negative aspects of the cross are embraced and accepted, then the possibility of authentic living is opened. If our society is going to be plunged into chaos and turmoil then triumphalistic answers will prove shallow. Those who urge on the revolution will find that they have betrayed their own past. In losing their ability to repent and grieve they will find they have lost their humanity. Those who have tried to shore up the defences of society will find themselves judged by those who could not live up to false standards. In terms of the Church's role within society the cross is not a banner to be waved in social or political causes, it is rather a judgement against any of these causes being identified with the coming kingdom. The Church must be freed, painfully, from its fantasies of power and influence in order to become what it is called to be—the common humanity which bears witness by its own suffering to the redemptive cross of Christ.

To follow that quotation with another, Canon A. M. Allchin wrote, in an article entitled 'The Holy Spirit in Christian Life', this of the solitary life:

> The life of the hermit reproduces in our own time the supreme paradox that it is in the moment of utmost isolation and complete apparent uselessness, in the desolation of the cross, that the Lord is able to bring about the atonement and reconciliation of man with God. We see here that the cross is lifegiving, and we see here something of the 'mounting of the cross' which is at the heart of monastic life.

(Sobornost, Summer 1966)

THE CALL TO THE SOLITARY LIFE WITHIN THE COMMUNITY OF THE
SISTERS OF THE LOVE OF GOD

In 1906 Father Hollings SSJE gathered into a tentative community
some women who desired to live the contemplative life, there being at that
time no Anglican contemplative community for men or women. After his
death in 1914 the guidance of the Sisters of the Love of God passed to
Father Lucius Cary SSJE who, like Father Hollings, would himself have
entered a contemplative community had one existed for men.

The original SLG Rule, drawn up by Father Hollings and later developed
and given more formal shape under the guidance of Father Cary, was not
a copy of any of the ancient Western Orders though, since Father Cary in
particular was steeped in the tradition of Carmel, the Rule had a decidedly
Carmelite flavour. The essential characteristic of the Community of the
Sisters of the Love of God is that from its foundation it has been free to
develop as circumstances and the growing life of the community should
dictate. From the very beginning there was a strong emphasis on the
solitary life of the cell as well as on the corporate life of liturgical worship
and work.

As the community continued to grow both in numbers and stability
there were some of its members who felt called by God to a greater degree
of silence and solitude, the first request being made in 1917—but it was
many years before the time seemed right to go forward into a permanent
venture for the whole Church.

In November 1963, Archimandrite Sophrony—himself at one time a
hermit on Mount Athos—came to visit Fairacres. With the full blessing of
the Archbishop of Canterbury, Father Gilbert Shaw, the Warden of the
community, and I sought counsel from the Orthodox tradition as to how
to form a settlement of solitaries, a *lavra*, the first members of which were
to be Sisters of the Love of God, trained for many years in the discipline
of the monastic life. We hoped that in time the settlement would become
ecumenical in character and be for laity and religious alike. While seeking
to learn from the Orthodox tradition our aim was to go back to the
fundamental experience of the early Church and the Fathers, Eastern and
Western, to discover how this ancient form of monastic eremitical life
could enrich and deepen our own Anglican recovery.

It was a memorable moment for both Father Shaw and myself when, after a long period of silence and prayer, Archimandrite Sophrony said: 'I believe this to be of the tradition and acceptable to God.' We both felt that the Holy Spirit had opened a door for the community into a further expression of the monastic life. The Community Council unanimously agreed in December of that year 'that the community was called to go beyond the question of temporary deserts for a few and to try to recover for the Church of England the fullness of the contemplative life in a settlement of solitaries'.

The vision finally became an actuality in May 1967 when the chapel and hermitages at Bede House, Staplehurst, Kent, were blessed by the Archbishop of Canterbury, though two of our Sisters had set forth in June of the preceding year to begin living their life there. The community was very much aware that our two Sisters were taking the whole body corporate with them into the desert; we did not think of them as going outside the community. Rather they were our ambassadors in the place of solitude to which God was calling them.

In the eremitical life there is no set pattern or mode of life. Each hermit will seek to follow the promptings of the Holy Spirit. Two of our Sisters have maintained their stability in the original lavra or skete; two returned to the cenobium for a further time before seeking and gaining permission to go into yet deeper silence and solitude. One Sister, after long years in the cenobium, was called to increasing silence and solitude without first experiencing the life of the lavra. Others have returned to the full cenobitic life after longer or shorter periods in the lavra.

TRAINING FOR THE SOLITARY LIFE

In his book, *The Call of the Desert*, Peter Anson wrote these wise words:

> There are always likely to be some men and women who feel that 'material' solitude is essential for their spiritual life. They can no more do without it than without food or drink, and if they are deprived of this isolation their lives become spoilt, cramped, and distorted, and they never find their true vocations. The 'born solitary' is drawn to an eremitical life for various reasons, partly natural, partly supernatural . . . They discover that they need to separate themselves from their fellow-creatures in order that their latent powers may have room for expansion and growth, that they may be more fitted so to serve mankind generally.
>
> (op. cit. SPCK, 1964, p. 212)

70

On the other hand, as an experienced Benedictine abbot has said, only twenty-five per cent of would-be hermits are likely to be genuine, but we must give an opportunity to the other seventy-five per cent who believe themselves to be called to the solitary life 'to test the spirits, whether they be of God'.

Though it would seem to be generally true that the cenobium should be the training ground for the solitary, it seems equally true that even if metanoia and the life of stability have not been firmly established, there are those who need to separate themselves from their fellow men in order that their latent powers of spirituality may, as Peter Anson says, have room for expansion and growth. The uniqueness of each personality whom God is recreating in the Spirit was deeply felt by Father Derwas Chitty. 'Be careful not to cramp the spirit,' he said. 'Because a Sister is difficult in the cenobium does not necessarily mean she is not ready for the solitary life. Only God can judge that.'

Thomas Merton has written that: 'The solitary should, with the blessing of the head of the monastery, be free to choose his own spiritual Father (Mother), but he will only deceive himself if, in making the choice, he seeks out a master who never tells him anything except what he wants to hear, and never commands him anything against his own will.' ('The Spiritual Father in the Desert Tradition', Thesis, February 1966.) It is obviously essential that the spiritual Father should have wise discernment and flexibility of mind to see God's will for the solitary at every stage of the response to God's call, and be like the Desert Fathers in their respect for the variety of personal vocations and 'ways'. Of the Desert Fathers Thomas Merton writes in the same work just quoted: 'They did not seek to impose hard and fast rules, reducing all to an arbitrary uniformity. Far from seeking security in a kind of servile conformity, they were able to appreciate the diversity of gifts which manifested the one Spirit.' The function of the spiritual Father must always be to encourage and guide the solitary more effectively to correspond to the divine call. The art of direction is never to dictate but to see Christ going before the soul, and to encourage each individual to respond with courage and generosity.

When the training of the solitary is under consideration it is important to emphasise that the foundations of ascetic discipline will usually have been laid in the faithful observance of life and prayer in the cenobium (monastery). The early Desert Fathers showed that the solitary life, except in the case of a special call from God, was fraught with danger unless there

71

was sufficient preparatory training, for 'if the mind desires to mount the cross before the senses have ceased from their sickness, the wrath of God comes upon it because it has entered upon a measure beyond its capacity'. (Abbot Isaias)

While obedience to the Spirit is the aim of the solitary, and must be formed and built up through his previous experience in the cenobium and through consultation with and obedience to others, to the tradition, and to the spiritual Father, yet obedience must be seen not as an end in itself but as a disposition of the will leading to that conformity with the will of God which is perfect freedom.

And with obedience on the one hand, there is need for penitence on the other and for the growing realisation of the solitary's own personal sinfulness. It is the call to satisfy the urge and thirst for God which will evoke from the heart the shedding of tears of compunction. There must first of all be the deeper solitude for repentance both for one's own sin and for the sin of the whole world; but the understanding of the meaning of sin arises out of the thirst and desire for God.

THE PRACTICE OF THE SOLITARY LIFE
General

Those early God-seekers of the fifth, sixth and seventh centuries lived many years in silence, wrestling with themselves as much as with God. They followed no written Rules—there were none. They recited psalmody by heart and those hearts were expanded by the interpretation of Holy Scripture as given to them by the staretz and by the tradition. They formulated no philosophy of life in those early days, and they certainly had no blueprint for a state of emerging embryonic monasticism.

The same applies to our modern hermits. We cannot hand then a blueprint of an exact timetable by which their way of prayer and the extent of the external activities they undertake should be carried out. Under the guidance of the Holy Spirit each one must find out what is the way for him; but at least we have the example of those early warriors for God in their lives of intense discipleship. They gave us a pattern of their experience in the *Apophthegmata Patrum*—the Sayings of the Fathers—and worth special mention are the works of Cassian. Some of these Sayings are prophetic, some obscure, some hortatory, some consolatory, some very severe and others very compassionate; but, as Archimandrite Barnabas has pointed out in an article, the personality of the speaker comes through in nearly every case, proving that the severe mode of life did not by any means destroy the nature of the person living it but, rather, transformed and transfigured him.

What then is the aim of the solitary? The solitary, having attained a certain degree of stability and having begun to know what silence is, may expect to be drawn deeper into the spiritual conflict. Archimandrite Barnabas, writing on his own experience of the eremitical life (*Fairacres Chronicle*, Spring 1975), wrote that 'it is as if the very setting up of a hermitage invites the close attention of the powers of good and evil, who play out their contest in the heart of the hermit'. He goes on: 'He will be plagued with memories, may even be drawn to daydreaming; as the novelty dies away he may suffer from boredom . . . then comes the temptation of '*Cui bono?*', does God really care? And as the purgative process continues . . . he will be led through successive waves of temptation; those that involve the faith, that attack hope, that corrupt love, and that assail the flesh, till he begins to realize that the famous diabolic attacks of St Antony were no exaggerated figments of the imagination . . .'

The conflict for the solitary will be to complete and to preserve peace in the self. There will still be assaults on the integrity of his response to personal unification, assaults from all that is as yet unreconciled in his own unconscious, as well as from external pressures or from the assaults of evil. But the solitary must renew his faith in God and set his will to possess and be possessed by God.

Only humility can give him that peace. Only in the strength of Christ's humility can the solitary sustain 'the dreadful searching of soul that strips him of his vanities and self-deceptions and can peacefully accept the fact that when his false ideas of himself are gone he has practically nothing else left. But then he is ready for the encounter with reality; the Truth and Holiness of God, which he must learn to confront in the depths of his own nothingness'. (Thomas Merton: *The Silent Life*)

It is through the perfection of his redirection of life that the solitary is made a peacemaker and can, as Father Gilbert Shaw wrote (*The Christian Solitary*), 'stand inviolate as a true icon of Christ's victory in the conflict with evil'.

The Timetable

The timetable of the solitary is a personal, individual thing, flexible yet under obedience to his spiritual Father. It will vary according to the spiritual maturity of the solitary and, on a practical level, quite often vary according to the season of the year, especially with regard to the rhythm of sleep and night prayer. The actual day will be divided into prayer and what may be termed 'prayerful activity'.

Prayer

The Eucharist will generally not be of daily necessity and, practically speaking, it may be an impossibility. 'Here before the altar,' writes Thomas Merton, 'where the community gathers for the eucharistic banquet, we know that the solitaries of the desert are also present. This is their Mass as well as ours . . . We remember finally that the whole body of monasticism past, present and to come, is there in a special way and that the entire Church is present, for it is her sacrifice.' (*The Silent Life*) Merton also tells us that while contemplation, like the other gifts of God is granted to souls as an outpouring of the infinite riches of God given to us in Christ in the Eucharist, the true fruition of the gift is not usually possible unless our eucharistic communion is somehow prolonged in silent and solitary adoration. He emphasises that the whole life of the hermit should be eucharistic in the sense of a life of praise and thanksgiving for the gifts of God.

This is a principle held consistently also by the Carthusians, but it is one which our present-day eucharistic theology finds it difficult to appreciate and apply to Christian practice. To quote again from Merton: 'His [the solitary's] chief function in the Church is not to celebrate the liturgical mysteries so much as to live, in silence and alone, the mystery of the Church's life "hidden with Christ in God". (Col. 3:3) . . . The heightened sense of unity in Christ is also the source of the hermit's eucharistic spirit and the fountain head of his thanksgiving.' (*The Silent Life*)

It follows, therefore, since the Office flows from the Eucharist, that there will be great variability as to how the Office is recited or offered. I know of one solitary who recites out loud, verse by verse, the whole Office by day and by night with all the appropriate bodily actions as in Choir. For another the Office may gradually become more interiorised so that the words of Scripture and psalmody are embodied by the Jesus Prayer or some other form of rhythmic prayer.

The prayer of the night will probably become increasingly meaningful and of necessity for most solitaries.

The whole being of the hermit must partake in the total offering to God and for mankind. Therefore, apart from the time of actual prayer, there must be a degree of exterior activity such as manual labour, housework, gardening, making of icons, weaving, translating, or any form of work consistent with solitude and which does not involve the breaking of the creative silence which is indispensible to his spiritual growth.

(Archimandrite Barnabas)

The more experienced solitary may, in this context, well have some form of apostolate by correspondence, or by giving spiritual counsel. As his life becomes increasingly purified, his passions stilled and his will more constantly attuned to the will of God, the hermit will be increasingly sensitive as to when charity should call him to break his silence and solitude. This involvement on the physical level will most likely be balanced by longer periods of even more complete withdrawal as, for example, in Advent and Lent, or when through his prayer he is drawn more deeply into the cosmic battle of the world's suffering, and participates in the victory of our Lord's reconciliation. Sister Adeline Cashmore, mentioned earlier, said when her spiritual Father commented on her fatigue, 'Yes, I am very weary. I have been drawn into the fringe of one of the Lord's battles and of his victory'. It is these times which will largely determine how frequently the hermit will wish to attend the Eucharist.

CONCLUSION

The hermit's way may be unintelligible to those not called to that life, and often part of the loneliness of the hermit is that, by the very nature of his calling, he cannot share with or explain to others the mystery of God's operations which are being revealed to him. This is the true loneliness of the desert and likewise the raw material of the spiritual warfare.

To sum up, the solitaries are the servants of the Church as the Church is the servant of the world. To them as to the Church is given the word of reconciliation and the ministry of reconciliation. They stand at the point of tension where the love of God and evil meet, to bear witness to stability in Christ. In the words of Gilbert Shaw: 'Cosmic prayer is the real prayer of the contemplative and of the solitary. It is prayer which realises that everything is being drawn together in a unity of proper relationship with God. It is the prayer of heaven, the prayer which the saints pray.'

The solitary, therefore, in his prayer is the most complete example of the coinherence of all mankind. Physically alone, isolated generally speaking from the centres where the majority of mankind lives out its human existence, he is at the heart of human experience, suffering, and relationship everywhere. Of the mode of his prayer it is impossible to speak, for each in his degree of openness to the Spirit's guiding will be drawn into Christ's reconciliation. What it is necessary to say is that whatever the rhythm of prayer may be, by day and by night, the solitary must never lose sight of the fact of Jesus as Saviour, and that it is he and only he who draws us to the Father and who has promised us the ministry of the Spirit. St John of the Cross explicitly says that we must never lose sight of the Incarnation and all that flows from it; that is the uniqueness and completeness of the Christian way.

In humility of spirit, the solitary knows that Divine Love waits for him in an abyss which as the years go on reveals even greater depths. He knows that his ordinary normal awareness is only part of a larger dimension, above, around, beneath his conscious being. It is an invitation to a battlefield, to new conflict. Seeing (vision) and worshipping is his work of reconciliation by which the world may draw out water from the wells of salvation. The conflict is at that point where vision clashes with the powers of evil. The way is not a kneeling before God with folded hands of supplication, but it is a going *into* God and there abiding so that he may flow out through us.

I should like to end with a final quotation from a paper called 'On the Desert Place of the Inner Sanctuary' (1974) by Raphael Vernay OSB:

> The hermit is simply a pioneer . . . in the way of the desert which the whole of humanity must follow of necessity one day, each one according to his measure and his desire. This eremitical vocation, at least embryonically, is to be found in every Christian vocation, but in some it must be allowed to come to its full flowering in the wind of the Spirit. It is not enough to affirm that the thing is good in itself, it is necessary that the Church and society do something, so that this life may be realizable, so that each may at least touch it, be it only with the tip of his little finger.

Is not this the purpose of our gathering here for the Church?

A STATEMENT ON THE SOLITARY LIFE

made at the conclusion of a meeting held at St David's, Wales

AN INFORMAL meeting to discuss the solitary life took place at St David's, Wales, from 29 September to 4 October 1975, bringing together twenty-six people representing the Roman Catholic, Orthodox, Anglican, and Congregationalist traditions. The members of the conference received the hospitality of the Passionist Fathers at St Non's and of the Sisters of the Anglican Community of St John the Evangelist, where their meetings were held. They were also able, through the kindness of the Dean and Chapter, to worship every day in the Cathedral Church, full of the memories of the saints of the first centuries of the Church in Wales.

The solitary life, lived in prayer and silence before God, which has never ceased to exist in the Christian East, is today being increasingly redis-covered in the Churches of the West. We rejoice at this movement as a sign of God's grace, and we believe that our common experience of the solitary vocation forms a strong bond of unity between our separated traditions.

During our discussion we gave particular consideration to the follow-ing points:

1) The life of solitude, while involving an external separation from society, is at the same time a life lived in profound communion with the whole Church and with all mankind. Dwelling 'on the frontier', separated from all, the solitary is at the same time united to all. Living often in conditions of the utmost simplicity and poverty, he or she is identified with all men in their need and poverty before God.

2) The solitary is called to experience with an especial directness the mystery of Christ's death and resurrection, into which all Christians are called to enter.

3) The existence of solitaries living geographically apart from society helps those living in society to realize the solitary dimension of their lives. In this way the solitary is a sign to the world, as well as to the Church. By virtue of its closeness to the material environment, the solitary life can help our present age to recover a more balanced relationship to the material world.

4) Today, as in the past, the solitary vocation assumes a very wide variety of forms; and in particular the degree of physical isolation can differ

greatly in individual instances. The *skete* or small fraternity of prayer and silence has an important role to play as a middle way between the community and the hermit.

5) This variety of forms means that an unusual degree of flexibility should be shown in the giving of spiritual direction to solitaries. The experience of the Orthodox Church suggests that it is not always necessary for the head of the community to be the director. While the solitary remains in obedience to the head of the community, the personal guidance of the solitary's inward life may sometimes be delegated to another.

6) The discernment of spirits is of the greatest importance in the recognition of the genuine vocation to solitude. It is evident that this is a way of life which demands considerable maturity, psychological as well as spiritual.

The spiritual richness we have found in these days together, suggests that this subject is one which needs further study, both historical and theological, and that there is the utmost value in small and informal gatherings in which experience of the life may be shared and evaluated.

André Louf
Abbot of Mont-des-Cats

Mother Mary Clare SLG Fairacres
Oxford.

Archimandrite Kallistos Ware
Oxford

A. M. Allchin

Canterbury.

APPENDIX

COMMUNAL SOLITUDE
THE SKETE FORM OF CHRISTIAN COMMUNITY*

THE WORD 'SKETE' would appear to be related to the word 'ascesis' and to mean a training place for the warfare of the spirit. It was first coined during the early stage of the monastic withdrawal movement in Egypt. West of the Nile delta, in the deserts of Nitria and Scetis, solitaries attracted disciples, who grouped themselves round an abba, or father—one who could guide and counsel and receive filial obedience. The sketes were usually quite small, just four or five men in each and sometimes no more than two. Every monk had his separate cell, often out of sight and sound of his neighbour. There was a small church for their daily or weekly common prayer, but most of the time was spent in solitude. There was also simple accommodation for visitors—of whom they often had more than they wanted!

The keynotes were: *obedience* above all; continual *attention to prayer and psalmody; manual work* as a discipline, and also to enable them to be self-supporting; and *hospitality*. No vows were taken but the growth into maturity and stability by perseverance was expected. There was no organisation except the arrangements for a common life. Each group was free to manage itself, and there appears to have been much interchange of visits between groups, although these were largely discouraged by the more discerning abbas.

These sketes were an alternative both to the completely solitary life of the heroic ascetics and to the completely common life of the huge, highly organised and military-like coenobium. Later on the large communities had dependent sketes of monks who were, and still remained, professed monks of the larger monasteries (as in Athos today). It was usually possible to remove to a skete under the direction and with the permission of the abbot and also, if he agreed, to a completely eremitic solitary life.

Forms of the skete life developed in the West also. For instance:

i) The small Celtic hermitage, often used by groups who would undertake missions from such a base.

ii) The eleventh-century Camaldolese adaptation of the Rule of Saint Benedict for small groups of hermits. This received an important

*Written by Roland Walls since the St David's Conference summarising briefly both theory and practice for those interested in this way.

79

new impetus under Paul Guistiniani in the sixteenth century at Monte Corona and is still in existence at Frascati, and in California and Ohio.

iii) Most of the major Orders also, at times, had dependent sketes, for instance, the Carmelites (who originally began as a group of sketes), and the Franciscans.

At the present time there is a remarkable revival of this form of life due to many reasons, among them the following:

i) The spirituality of Charles de Foucauld and of the Little Brothers and Sisters of Jesus has recovered the virtue of littleness in a life of prayer lived in the polarity of solitude and urban society.

ii) The close contacts now being established with the Eastern Orthodox tradition, and a new understanding of the ethos of the Desert Fathers.

iii) The need for the highly organised Orders in the Roman and Anglican Churches to reconsider the essentials of the monastic life.

iv) The need of the whole Church to recover the simplicity and humanity of its form of life in the world.

Adapatations of this style of life to present conditions need great care to preserve the true tradition of the skete as a genuine form of the religious life. Normally a skete grows out of a coenobitic community whose members have already learnt the discipline of prayer and obedience. The skete is born out of the community's need to have a nursery for vocations to the semi-solitary life, or as part of its own life where temporary long retreats under family conditions can be encouraged. Because the skete needs to be grounded in obedience, a group which grows into a skete without the usual prelude of training in a larger community will need to have the closest association with one. This larger community would normally provide it with a director. Such a skete would also have to take care that its relation to the Church was assured by putting itself under the aegis of the bishop or some other recognised Church authority. Anything like the wrong sort of independence, or group self-pleasing, would defeat the skete's essential grounding in obedience and its calling to live at the heart of the Church. The skete is not so much an alternative form of the religious life as a development from its present forms and a return to an unbroken tradition. The freedom grows out of obedience and has nothing to do with the freedom of self-determination.

Practically, a skete can be sited either in a rural retreat or in, or near, an urban centre. It needs at least a small garden enclosure. It can, and perhaps should, be self-supporting, with members taking turns to work part-time in jobs outside if no home industry is possible. The skete will provide simple hospitality for one or two at a time, especially for the poor and distressed.

Among the advantages of the skete form of life are the following: It allows for the combination of solitude, community and openness to society under obedience. There is the possibility for a brother, if so called, to live the completely solitary life in dependence on the skete. And it encourages the simplicity of a family, in which the unselfconscious humanity of the brothers is all-important as they receive the people God sends to them. The form of life itself underlines the need for poverty of possessions and poverty of spirit.

THE SKETE AND ORDERED SOLITUDE
OTIOSUM NEGOTIUM

THE SKETE form of life places a great deal of responsibility on each brother as to how he spends his time when solitary. This life of community and solitude, therefore, requires a cell discipline undertaken by each brother, drawn up to suit his needs, and with the advice of the community. The cell rule is a guide to obedience in solitude, and is useful in picking up a programme of solitude, however short, for any brother whose work has taken him away from the house. Thus the communal rule of the skete, and the cell discipline, together enable the brothers to see obedience as the central feature of a dedicated life. Brothers are naturally free to experiment with the details of the cell discipline, but a longish period has been found to be needed before the effects can be judged, usually a month or so at least.

Advice and direction is sought for any changes. Sketes vary considerably in how much of the Divine Office is said communally and how much is said by each brother on his own. They vary too in their requirements for weekdays and Sundays and festivals, the communal activities sometimes being stepped up at weekends and feasts. The skete has therefore a great deal of flexibility built into it so that each brother, and the whole little community, can grow in a freedom of service where discipline does not require regimentation, and needs and changes due to age or development can be allowed for.

In conclusion it needs to be said that the skete form of life *per se* is not better than any other form of life; it is simply the right form of life for those who are called to it. *All* will arrive at the 'top of the mountain of vision' who in truth of heart seek God, as Fr. Augustine Baker says in the following passage:

> It is an illustrious proof of the abundant, most communicative, over-flowing riches of the divine goodness to all His servants whatsoever that in truth of heart seek Him, that this state of contemplation . . . should neither be enclosed only in caverns, rocks, or deserts, nor fixed to solitary religious communities, nor appropriated to the subtlety of wit, profoundest of judgement, gifts of learning or study, etc.; but that the poorest, simplest soul living in the world, and following the common life of good Christians there, if she will faithfully correspond to the internal light and tracts afforded her by God's Spirit, may as securely, yea, and sometimes more speedily, arrive to the top of the mountain of vision than the most learned doctors, the most profoundly wise men, yea, the most . . . confined hermits.

From the treatise 'All Conditions capable of Contemplation' in
Holy Wisdom (Burns & Oates, 1964) p.106

ROSLIN
All Saints 1976

SELECT BOOK LIST

Early Monasticism

Owen Chadwick, *Western Asceticism*, SCM Press 1958.

Sister Benedicta Ward SLG, *The Wisdom of the Desert Fathers*, from the Anonymous Series, SLG Press 1975.

Sister Benedicta Ward SLG, *The Sayings of the Desert Fathers*, the Alphabetical Collection. Mowbrays 1975.

Saint Athanasius, *Life of Saint Antony*, trans. R. T. Meyer in Ancient Christian Writers. Washington 1950.

Palladius, *The Lausiac History*, Ancient Christian Writers. Longman, Green 1965.

St John Climacus, *The Ladder of Divine Ascent*, trans. Archimandrite Lazarus Moore, Faber 1959.

Early Fathers from the Philokalia, trans. E. Kadloubovsky and G.E.H. Palmer, Faber 1954.

Writings from the Philokalia on Prayer of the Heart, trans. Kadloubovsky and Palmer. Faber 1951.

Derwas J. Chitty, *The Desert a City*, Basil Blackwell, 1966.

Owen Chadwick, *John Cassian: A Study in Primitive Monasticism*, Cambridge 1968.

Cuthbert Butler, *Benedictine Monachism*, Cambridge 1961.

Medieval to Modern

William of St-Thierry, *The Golden Epistle*, Cistercian Fathers Series, Spencer , Mass. USA 1971.

J. Leclercq, *Alone with God* A guide to the hermit way of life based on the teachings of Blessed Paul Giustiniani, Hodder & Stoughton 1962.

P. F. Anson, *The Call of the Desert*, SPCK 1964.

Thomas Merton, *The Power and Meaning of Love*, Sheldon Press 1976. (Formerly called *Disputed Questions*—see note 10 on p.16. The essay in this book, 'The Philosophy of Solitude' is exceptionally fine.)

Archimandrite Sophrony, *The Monk from Mount Athos* and *Wisdom of Mount Athos*. Both Mowbrays 1973.

Gilbert Shaw, *The Christian Solitary* (pamphlet), SLG Press 1969.

André Louf, *Teach us to Pray*, Darton, Longman & Todd 1974.

There are many books on this subject in French. Among them see *Femmes au Désert* by Marie Le Roy Ladurie, Éditions Saint-Paul, Paris-Fribourg 1971.

A. M. ALLCHIN, since 1973 a Canon of Canterbury. His first published work, *The Silent Rebellion* (1958), was an account of the revival of the Religious Life in the Church of England in the nineteenth century. Since then he has published a number of articles on monastic themes. He is Warden of the Community of the Sisters of the Love of God.

DOM ANDRÉ LOUF, since 1963 Abbot of the Cistercian monastery of Mont des Cats in Northern France. Well known in France and the Low Countries as a spiritual guide and teacher, whose doctrine is inspired by the Fathers of East and West as well as by the great Cistercian founders, his book, *Teach Us To Pray*, has begun to make him equally well known in the English speaking world.

ARCHIMANDRITE KALLISTOS (TIMOTHY) WARE, monk of the Monastery of St John the Theologian, Patmos, Greece; since 1966 priest in charge of the Greek Orthodox parish of the Holy Trinity, Oxford. Fellow of Pembroke College, Oxford, and Spalding Lecturer in Eastern Orthodox Studies. Author of *The Orthodox Church* (Pelican Books); editor of *The Art of Prayer: An Orthodox Anthology*; co-translator of *The Festal Menaion*.

ROLAND WALLS trained for the priesthood at Kelham; was a novice of SSM 1949-51, Fellow of Corpus Christi College, Cambridge, 1948-1962, and Chaplain and Dean of Chapel, 1953-1958. Taught theology at Edinburgh University, 1963-1974. Now at Roslin where the 'skete' Community of the Transfiguration began in 1965. Emerges occasionally to give retreats and conferences on the life of prayer.

SISTER BENEDICTA WARD is a member of the Community of the Sisters of the Love of God. She has published several articles on medieval and monastic themes and three volumes of translations of medieval and patristic texts (*The Prayers and Meditations of St Anselm, The Sayings of the Desert Fathers,* and *The Wisdom of the Desert Fathers*).

MOTHER MARY CLARE is the ex-Mother General of the Community of the Sisters of the Love of God. She held Office as Superior from 1954-1973 during which time eremitical vocations within the Community developed and are being lived out both at Bede House, Kent, and in North Wales.

FAIRACRES PUBLICATIONS

BY GILBERT SHAW

ALL TITLES LISTED ABOVE ARE OBTAINABLE—POSTAGE EXTRA—FROM:

SLG PRESS

CONVENT OF THE INCARNATION

FAIRACRES   OXFORD

OX4 1TB

Price List March 1977